22 DAYS IN THE AMERICAN SOUTHWEST

THE ITINERARY PLANNER
SECOND EDITION

RICHARD HARRIS

John Muir Publications
Santa Fe, New Mexico

Other books by Richard Harris
22 Days in Florida
22 Days in the Pacific Northwest

This book is for Rita Guidi-Morosini, artist, environmental activist, and steady source of insight and inspiration.

Special thanks to those who make it possible, including the Rio Grande chapter of the Sierra Club, Pamela Lanier and Julio Valdez, Anne Wright, Richard Polese, and the National Park Service.

John Muir Publications, P.O. Box 613, Santa Fe, NM 87504

Second edition. Second printing April 1991

Library of Congress Cataloging-in-Publication Data
Harris, Richard, 1947-
    22 days in the American Southwest: the itinerary planner/
Richard Harris. — 2nd ed.
        p. cm — (JMP travel)
    ISBN 0-945465-49-1
    1. Southwest, New—Description and travel—1981- — Tours.
I. Title. II. Title: Twenty-two days in the American Southwest.
III. Series.
F787.H36 1990
917.904'33—dc20   90-35333
                                                             CIP

Distributed to the book trade by:
W. W. Norton & Company, Inc.
New York, New York

Design Mary Shapiro
Maps Holly Wood
Cover Map Michael Taylor
Typography Copygraphics, Inc., Santa Fe, N.M.
Printer McNaughton & Gunn, Inc.

CONTENTS

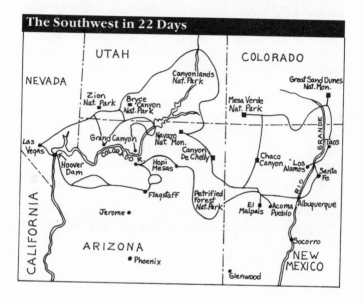

The Southwest in 22 Days

HOW TO USE THIS BOOK

Under the ancient volcano in northern New Mexico lives the nation's largest community of nuclear physicists. Twelve miles to the east, the people of San Ildefonso Pueblo speak their Native American language, dance in time-honored ceremonies, and make pottery by methods a thousand years old. Five miles to the south, in the Bandelier wilderness, you can walk for three days without coming to a road.

Welcome to the American Southwest, where pristine wilderness and civilizations many centuries old endure side by side with "Star Wars" technology. *22 Days in the American Southwest* contains a self-guided travel itinerary for a three-week road trip that will take you to the most fascinating places in New Mexico, Arizona, and the southern parts of Colorado, Utah, and Nevada. The tour follows a 3,000-mile meandering loop, mostly on less-used secondary highways. It intersects Interstate 40 several times and connects with Interstates 15, 25, and 70, so it's easy to join and leave from any direction.

If you have less than three weeks to explore, use any of the route's various segments as a relaxing scenic alternative to I-40. These segments range from a few hours to a week or more. The tour takes you to seven national parks, twelve national monuments, and assorted state parks, national forests, and BLM scenic areas. You'll also visit the lands of the Pueblo, Hopi, Zuñi, and Navajo people, as well as two of America's most unusual—even improbable—cities, Santa Fe and Las Vegas.

The itinerary strikes a balance between the region's famous, often crowded tourist meccas and more serene places where sightseers rarely venture. For example, you can join the throng ogling the Grand Canyon from the lodge patio; but, in case solitude suits your personal travel style better, I'll also share my own secret spot where you can camp in privacy right on the Grand Canyon rim, no ranger on duty, for free.

The itinerary format in this book is divided into 22 daily sections, containing:

1. A **suggested schedule** for each day's travel and sightseeing.

2. A detailed **travel route** description for each driving segment of your trip.

3. **Descriptive overviews** and **sightseeing highlights** (rated in order of importance: ▲▲▲ Don't miss; ▲▲ Try hard to see; and ▲ See if you get a chance).

4. A **suggested campground** for each night of the trip, as well as **restaurant and lodging recommendations** for those who choose not to camp.

5. **Helpful hints**—random tidbits that will help make your trip go well.

6. **Itinerary options**—excursion suggestions for travelers who have extra time.

7. User-friendly **maps** designed to show you what the road up ahead is really like.

Why 22 Days?

"22 Days" itinerary guidebooks like this one started in 1985 with Rick Steves' *Europe in 22 Days*, a do-it-yourself alternative to organized three-week bus tours. The series now includes such diverse destinations as Mexico, Australia, and India. You wouldn't dream of touring Europe or India in less than three weeks, because you may only have that single chance to experience what you'll remember for the rest of your life.

I invite you to explore America with the same "once in a lifetime" enthusiasm. You can see the Southwest in three weeks, for just slightly more money than you'd spend if you stayed home, and the experience will rival any foreign vacation.

Recently I commented to a ranger on the surprising number of European tourists visiting the national park where he worked. "You bet," he agreed. "Frenchmen know a lot more about this part of the country than most Americans do."

My experience verified this as I recalled working my way through college as a Pikes Peak tour guide. Every week, tourists from east of the Mississippi, where states are smaller, would tell me their trip plans: go up Pikes Peak this morning, drive on and see the Grand Canyon this afternoon, spend the night in Vegas (tomorrow it's on to Disneyland). Twelve Hours in the American Southwest. Maybe some of them accomplished it, too, back when many western highways had no speed limits. It's just that they didn't see very much.

The Southwest is vast. Distance isolates. The isolation protects ancient Native American traditions and Spanish colonial heritage. Some parts of the region remain completely uninhabited. There are roadless areas larger than some eastern states. The same vastness that makes the Southwest so alluring can isolate you behind a windshield, watching those green and white interstate signs that all look the same from coast to coast—except that out here they beckon to strange-sounding places like "Ácoma Sky City," "Shungopavi," and "Zyzyx Road." The heartland of the American Southwest ranks among the most wild and exotic places on earth. Take time to explore!

You don't even need a passport.

How Much Will It Cost?

I've taken this 22-day trip in comfort, driving a moderate-size RV with a Dodge V-8 engine, on a $1,000 trip budget, returning home with eight new pieces of Indian jewelry and twenty-one dollars in cash.

The major expense of the trip is gasoline. Figure 3,000 miles plus the round-trip driving distance from your home to the most convenient point on the tour route, at however many miles per gallon your rig gets.

If you cook your own meals, they'll cost the same as you'd spend eating at home. If you prefer the convenience of eating out, allow $5 per person per meal.

There are only six towns on this 22-day trip where you can find a more expensive restaurant if you want one.

I have tried to include lodging suggestions in all price ranges when possible. In some places along this route, there are no budget motels; in other places, there are no expensive ones. If you plan to take this trip without ever camping out, budget $40 to $50 per night for lodging.

Public campground fees average $7 to $8 per night. National forests and Arizona and New Mexico state parks charge $7; Utah state parks charge $8. Most national parks and monuments charge $5 to camp, plus the admission charge. There are also abundant possibilities for free camping.

Admission to state parks, national monuments, and national parks is typically $5 per vehicle. An annual Golden Eagle Pass, admitting you to all U.S. national parks and monuments free, is a sound investment on this trip.

Souvenirs, particularly Native American arts and crafts, will tempt you to spend whatever is left of your vacation budget. I suggest that you go ahead and spend it among the Indians. Otherwise, the casino operators of Las Vegas will be waiting for you, and those guys are professionals at the art of separating tourists from their money.

When to Go
The best season for sightseeing in the Southwest is between May 1 and October 15. Before Memorial Day or after Labor Day, you can avoid crowds and extreme heat. Late spring travel reveals the desert in full bloom, while early autumn paints the mountainsides in aspen gold. However, summer travel gives you more hours of daylight, extra time to enjoy the desert at sunset and in the early morning.

Some destinations in this book, including the Grand Canyon North Rim, close in the winter. Most campgrounds are also closed. Sudden snowstorms can interrupt your trip at any point. Yet winter sports enthusiasts will discover fine ski slopes with remarkably short lift

lines as well as excellent cross-country ski trails and
plenty of sunshine.

Other places in the Southwest, such as Phoenix, Tucson, the lower Colorado River, and the Sonora Desert are
left out of the 22-day itinerary simply because they're too
hot to even consider visiting in the summer months. In
winter, though, these areas are warm, dry, and pleasant.

The only impossibly hot place I've included in this
itinerary is the Las Vegas/Lake Mead area, where you can
beat the midday 100-degree heat with indoor sightseeing
or a visit to the beach.

Transportation

Seeing the Southwest by train and bus is possible and
enjoyable but restricting. You can only get to the majority
of places in this book by private vehicle.

I recommend a camper truck, van conversion, or small
motor home for this trip, but a sporty convertible or a station wagon full of kids will do fine. You won't need four-
wheel drive, though you will sometimes find yourself
driving on well-maintained unpaved roads. I've included
only those roads where I've personally seen large RVs go.
If you have a motor home the size of a Greyhound bus,
you'll need a bit of hubris but not the AAA tow truck.

Whatever vehicle you drive, be sure that it's sound
enough to purr along through 3,000 miles of varied driving conditions includudg hot temperatures, high alti-
tudes, and steep grades—or at least that you're equipped
to handle roadside breakdowns when the nearest telephone or service station is 60 miles away. Be sure the
spare tire and jack are in good condition, and carry a gallon of radiator coolant. For the confidence that comes
from being ready for anything, take spare V-belts and
radiator hoses as well as a basic automotive tool kit and
an automotive repair manual.

RV Rentals

A growing number of visitors to the Southwest, notably
European tourists, choose to fly into a western hub city

like Albuquerque or Phoenix, then rent a motor home to explore more remote places where public transportation can't take them.

Many motor home dealers also act as rental agencies, representing owners who want to rent out their RVs when they're not using them, or call CruiseAmerica, (800) 327-7778, for nationwide round-trip and one-way RV rental information. Two dealers in Albuquerque who rent RVs are Bob Myers RV Center, 12024 Central Avenue SE, (505) 298-7961, and Wayne's Recreational Vehicles, 12020 Central Avenue SE, (505) 296-0505. Rental rates vary widely, from $275 to $500 per week for van-length RVs and from $500 to $800 per week for big motor homes. It pays to shop around.

Renting an RV will cost more than all other expenses of your southwestern trip combined. If tight-budget travel is your plan, buy a tent instead. However, the luxury and comfort of motor home adventuring will cost no more than a student-style tour of Europe. It's particularly worth the extra cost if you're a newcomer to the world of RV travel and want to try one out on an extended trip before buying your own. Besides the hands-on experience, you can get ample advice about "rigs" from your neighbors in campgrounds everywhere. It's the ultimate icebreaker and a major topic of conversation.

RVs available for rent range in size from cramped to palatial. For this trip I suggest a modest size, preferably what is often called a "mini motor home," a custom-built living area mounted on a van-length frame. The places mentioned in this book can be reached even in a mammoth two-bedroom land yacht. Gas consumption will be alarming, and so will wear and tear on the driver's nerves. A big motor home is a wise choice, though, for families of four or more. It's true, you can sleep six in a mini motor home, but by Day 6 of this trip you may experience an almost overwhelming urge to leave the kids playing video games in a truck stop while you hop in your rig and hightail it for the state line.

Food and Lodging

Tent or RV, this itinerary assumes you're equipped to camp, at least part of the time. Fine hotels and restaurants are a big industry in some southwestern communities such as Santa Fe and Las Vegas, but for more than half of this trip, camping is the best way. On much of the route, food and lodging establishments are few, far between, and not luxurious.

My primary suggestion for each night is a public campground. When possible, I've picked campgrounds where the amenities include good rest rooms, evening walking trails, and slide shows by the campfire—all for a fraction of the cost of a room with TV at a ma-and-pa highway motel.

Anyone—casual tent camper, long-term motor home traveler, or seasoned backpacker—can develop a sudden yearning for a comfortable room with a hot shower and a telephone. This book describes alternate lodging suggestions that range from the basic necessities to big-splurge elegance. Tenderfoot noncampers can go the whole route without sleeping outdoors. When intriguing possibilities arise—bed and breakfasts, historic hotels, national park lodges, or casino hotels—I'll give you enough details so that you can make advance reservations. Otherwise, I'll direct you to the nearest town offering reasonably priced motels.

Nearby towns are also the place to find groceries or, if you must, a cheeseburger deluxe with fries or a Mexican combination plate. Where gourmet grocery shopping or local produce is available, I'll let you know. Sometimes regional food specialties make restaurant dining a vacation highlight; I'll show you the best places to find New Mexican green chile stew, Navajo fry bread, and Las Vegas bargain breakfasts as well as sunny-side up eggs overlooking the Grand Canyon.

Recommended Reading

22 Days in the American Southwest gives you the opportunity to see a kaleidoscope of cultures and wilderness panoramas. The more you know about them, the more you'll enjoy them. In this slim guide I can only tell you enough to whet your enthusiasm. Here are my favorite regional books, both fiction and nonfiction, available in most New Mexico and Arizona bookstores.

Charles Lummis's vivid and evocative *The Land of Poco Tiempo*, written in 1893, contains descriptions of life among the Norteño, Pueblo, and Apache people which remain surprisingly accurate nearly a century later. Also of interest is *The Delight Makers*, a novel of prehistoric Pueblo Indian life by Lummis's friend, archaeologist Adolph Bandelier.

Santa Fe's long, rich history is dramatized in a mini-Micheneresque saga entitled *The Centuries of Santa Fe* by Paul Horgan, lavish with accurate details on New Mexican life from early Spanish conquistadores to World War II. Those interested in the early years of Santa Fe's Anglo artist colony will enjoy *Artists of the Canyons and Caminos* by Edna Robertson and Sarah Nestor.

Los Alamos' Manhattan Project and its impact on neighboring communities is the subject of Frank Waters's classic *The Woman at Otowi Bridge* as well as a recent popular thriller, *Stallion Gate*, by Martin Cruz Smith.

Life in the Spanish villages of northern New Mexico is beautifully portrayed in *Bless Me, Ultima*, an autobiographical novel by University of New Mexico professor Rudolfo Anaya. For a broader, more offbeat view of the arrival of the twentieth century in northern New Mexico, read three big novels by Taos area author John Nichols: *The Milagro Beanfield War, The Magic Journey,* and *The Nirvana Blues*. The motion picture version of *The Milagro Beanfield War*, available on videocassette, may well be the best film portrayal ever of the people and problems of northern New Mexican villages.

Shelves full of books are available on the Navajo, from Navajo-English dictionaries to epic translations of Navajo song cycles. Good histories of the tribe include *The Navajo Nation* by Peter Iverson and the more readable *The Navajos* by Ruth M. Underhill. Among several accounts of traditional Navajo life told to early-twentieth-century anthropologists, my favorite is *Son of Old Man Hat*, recorded in 1934 by National Research Council Fellow Walter Dyk.

University of New Mexico journalism professor Tony Hillerman's unique mystery novels about the Navajo Tribal Police—*Skinwalkers, The Ghostway, The Dark Wind, People of Darkness, Listening Woman, Dance Hall of the Dead,* and *The Blessing Way*—offer vivid, accurate insights into modern Navajo life. Read any of them and discover why they are perennial best-sellers in southwestern bookstores. His most recent novel, *A Thief of Time*, is set partly in Chaco Canyon and deals with archaeology and pothunting among the Anasazi ruins.

If I had to choose just one book for spare-time reading on this tour, it would be *Desert Solitaire*, the late Edward Abbey's memoir of a season as a ranger in Arches National Monument during the late 1950s. This collage of nature lore, environmental politics, and wilderness adventure is set in Moab, Arches, Canyonlands, Lake Powell, Capitol Reef, the Grand Canyon, and Supai. Abbey's novel, *The Monkey Wrench Gang*, a cult classic among environmental activists, inspired the popular southwestern pastime of "wrenching" (defending the environment by sabotage). Abbey's last novel, published in 1990, was a sequel to *The Monkey Wrench Gang* entitled *Hayduke Lives!*

The Exploration of the Colorado River and Its Canyons by Maj. John Wesley Powell is a record of the first expedition (1869) by river through the Grand Canyon—using wooden boats. Other enjoyable Grand Canyon classics include Joseph Wood Krutch's *Grand Canyon* and Colin Fletcher's *The Man Who Walked Through Time*.

Where to Start

22 Days in the American Southwest is a loop trip. You can start anywhere on the circle.

Albuquerque, the interstate highway system's major southwestern crossroads (I-25 north-south, I-40 east-west), is the ideal starting point for this trip if you're coming from Texas or points north or east. Albuquerque International Airport is convenient for those who plan to fly to the Southwest and then rent a vehicle.

If you're coming from the southern parts of California or Arizona, join this route on I-40 at Kingman, Arizona (Day 17), and follow the circle around (going from Day 22 to Day 1) to end your tour in Las Vegas (Day 16).

Coming from the Bay Area, northern California, or the Pacific Northwest, augment the tour by crossing the Sierras through Yosemite National Park, going south through Death Valley National Monument, starting and finishing this "22 Days" route in Las Vegas.

Interstate Alternatives

For readers with less time and those en route to someplace else, segments of this tour can be adapted as relaxing scenic alternatives to I-40, ranging from a few hours to more than a week:

■ Between Albuquerque, and Grants or Gallup, New Mexico, explore northern New Mexico, southern Colorado, and Anasazi country (Days 1 to 7).

■ Between Gallup, New Mexico, and Kingman, Arizona (also intersecting I-70 at Green River and St. George, Utah), travel through Hopi and Navajo reservations, Utah national parks, and Las Vegas (Days 8 to 17).

■ Between Kingman and Flagstaff, Arizona, take old Route 66 (Day 17) instead of the interstate.

■ Between Flagstaff and Holbrook, visit the Grand Canyon and Hopi mesas (Days 19 and 20).

■ Between Holbrook, Arizona, and Grants, New Mexico, visit Petrified Forest National Park, the Zuñi Reservation, El Morro, and El Malpais (Days 21 and 22).

Sightseeing highlights you can see along I-40 without major detours are those in the Albuquerque/Santa Fe area (Days 1 and 2), the Grants area (Day 6), Petrified Forest National Park (Day 7), and Flagstaff (Days 17 and 18).

In addition, travelers with limited time can abbreviate this tour into a two-week trip by jumping from Page (Day 13) to Tuba City (Day 20), an hour's drive via US 89 south and US 160 east. It's also an easy one-hour trip between Gallup (Day 8) and Grants (Days 21 and 22), a useful shortcut for splitting this itinerary into two separate trips—a New Mexico tour and an around-the-Grand Canyon tour.

The itinerary in this book is flexible. Tailor it to fit your own time frame.

Time Zones

Practically all of this tour takes place in the Rocky Mountain time zone, but during daylight saving months keeping your wristwatch correct isn't as easy as it sounds. Arizona (except for the Navajo Reservation), does not observe daylight saving time, so New Mexico and Arizona times are different in the summer, except on the Navajo Reservation, which observes daylight saving time on both sides of the state line. To keep things simple, all Suggested Schedule times in this book assume daylight saving time. If you never reset your watch, everything will work out fine.

22 Days in the American Southwest

DAY 1 In Albuquerque, New Mexico, drive or ride the aerial tramway to the top of Sandia Crest to view the land you'll be exploring during the next week. Other Albuquerque attractions include the Pueblo Indian Cultural Center and ancient petroglyphs at the edge of modern suburbs.

DAY 2 Follow the Turquoise Trail to Santa Fe, New Mexico. Spend the day visiting museums, churches, and art galleries in Santa Fe's historic plaza district as well as Indian and folk art museums.

DAY 3 En route to Bandelier National Monument, visit Shidoni's sculpture garden, San Ildefonso Pueblo, and Los Alamos. Day hike in Bandelier or explore by car higher in the Jemez Mountains.

DAY 4 Take the High Road to Taos through traditional Spanish villages, then descend into the Rio Grande Gorge. After visiting Taos, continue north into Colorado to Great Sand Dunes National Monument.

DAY 5 Play among the sand dunes. Then drive to Durango and Mesa Verde National Park. Choose either the direct route over Wolf Creek Pass or the less traveled, even more scenic route through Cumbres and Chama.

DAY 6 Visit America's largest—and most popular—cliff dwellings at Mesa Verde National Park.

DAY 7 Today's trip takes you to two other 800-year-old Anasazi cities: Aztec Ruins and isolated Chaco Canyon, the largest pueblo city ever built.

DAY 8 Return from Chaco Canyon to I-40 near Gallup, New Mexico. Drive on to the Navajo Reservation, where you'll visit the Navajo Tribal Zoo and Hubbell Trading Post, ending the day at Canyon de Chelly.

DAY 9 Travel from Canyon de Chelly to Monument Valley, with an optional detour to Navajo National Monument, site of the Anasazi cliff dwellings, Betatakin and Keet Seel. At Monument Valley Tribal Park, visit traditional Navajo homes amid landscapes familiar from cowboy movies.

DAY 10 Heading into Utah, follow the Trail of the Ancients with a morning hiking break at Natural Bridges National Monument. Continue north to the town of Moab and Canyonlands National Park's Island in the Sky.

DAY 11 Three national parks in one day: awaken in Canyonlands and get an early start to tour Arches, then drive southwest, arriving at Capitol Reef in time to enjoy the cool of the evening in Utah's least-known national park.

DAY 12 From Capitol Reef to Bryce Canyon, by way of Escalante Canyons, is one of the most beautiful stretches of road on this tour. At busy Bryce Canyon National Park, take an easy walk along the canyon rim or a more demanding one down among the hoodoos.

DAY 13 Take a scenic detour to Glen Canyon Dam and spend the night at Lee's Ferry, where the Grand Canyon begins.

DAY 14 Spend a day and night on the North Rim of the Grand Canyon.

DAY 15 Travel from the Grand Canyon through Zion National Park, then take I-15 to Las Vegas. Rather than rush into the city, why not enjoy a peaceful desert night in the Valley of Fire?

DAY 16 Bright lights, noise, glitz, greed, and fast money round the clock: experience Las Vegas. Approach the city by the scenic route along the Lake Mead shore to Hoover Dam. Swim and sunbathe at a desert beach.

DAY 17 Drive from Las Vegas to Flagstaff by either I-40 or old Route 66.

DAY 18 Keep the same campsite or motel room. Within a few minute's drive of the city limits, sightseeing highlights include Walnut Canyon National Monument, Lowell Observatory, and the Museum of Northern Arizona.

DAY 19 Return to the Grand Canyon, this time visiting the South Rim. On the way there, see Sunset Crater and Wupatki national monuments.

DAY 20 Drive across the desert of the western Navajo Reservation to one of the most remote places in the United States, the ancient group of villages on top of the Hopi mesas.

DAY 21 Cross I-40 at Petrified Forest National Park, with its red, white, and blue painted desert. Then drive through the Zuñi Reservation to El Morro National Monument, the nation's first.

DAY 22 Around Grants, New Mexico, visit El Malpais National Monument and Ácoma Pueblo. You're now just a one-hour drive from Albuquerque, where this tour began three weeks ago.

ALBUQUERQUE

At the crossroads of two interstate highways and with the state's only major commercial airport, Albuquerque is the natural place to begin a tour of northern New Mexico and the Four Corners area.

Before World War II, Albuquerque was a sleepy little university town about the same size as Santa Fe. Its strategic location at the intersection of I-25 and I-40 explains why the city is approaching half a million in population, while other New Mexican towns remain small. All streets are designated by quadrant. For example, if you're on Lomas Boulevard NE, you are north of I-40 and east of I-25. It's hard to get lost as long as you remember that Sandia Crest, the big mountain nearby, is to the east.

Suggested Schedule

10:00 a.m.	Drive to Petroglyph Park on the city's west edge.
10:30 a.m.	Walk through Petroglyph Park.
11:00 a.m.	Return to I-40 and drive to the Pueblo Cultural Center.
11:30 a.m.	Visit the Pueblo Cultural Center. Eat lunch at the restaurant there.
1:00 p.m.	Drive to the Sandia Tramway station.
1:30 p.m.	Ride the tramway to Sandia Crest.
2:00 p.m.	Hike Sandia Crest.
4:00 p.m.	Descend from the mountain.
4:30 p.m.	Visit Old Town, a good area for strolling and dining.

Sightseeing Highlights

▲▲ **Petroglyph Park**—West Mesa Escarpment, the cliff below the small, extinct volcanoes on the horizon, defines the western edge of Albuquerque. Housing subdivisions sprawl up to the base of the escarpment; from the top rim, the land is empty and almost roadless for a hundred miles to the west, home only to jackrabbits and coyotes. The black volcanic boulders tumbled all along the escarpment contain over 15,000 pre-Columbian Indian petroglyphs—more than at any other site in the United States. Much of this rock art dates back a thousand years or more.

In 1988, the federal government decided to declare a large area of the West Mesa Escarpment a national monument, but there was a catch: the city of Albuquerque and the state of New Mexico would have to contribute part of the money to purchase the land from private landowners. So far, the funds have not been available, and development pressures are now creating doubts as to whether the proposed national monument will ever become a reality. You can see a tiny sampling of the rock art by climbing the trail through municipal Petroglyph Park.

The meanings of some of the petroglyphs, such as animal pictures, are self-evident, and anthropologists have interpreted some of the abstract symbols with the help of modern-day Rio Grande Pueblo people, whose ancient ancestors chipped them into the rocks. Some of the figures remain mysterious. Notice the images of Kokopelli, the hunchbacked flute player thought to symbolize fertility, which are common throughout the Anasazi country in New Mexico, Colorado, Utah, and Arizona. Humanlike horned figures may represent prehistoric shamans. Early Spanish settlers believed that they were devils and carved crosses near them to neutralize their supposed black magic powers.

To reach Petroglyph Park, take I-40 west and turn off northbound at Coors Road, exit 155. Veer left and follow Atrisco Road to the park.

▲▲ **Indian Pueblo Cultural Center**—Owned by the Native American Pueblos of New Mexico, this cultural center has a series of galleries selling Indian arts and crafts in all price ranges surrounding the central open-air dance plaza, as well as a museum. Indian dances and craft demonstrations are held here on most weekends during the

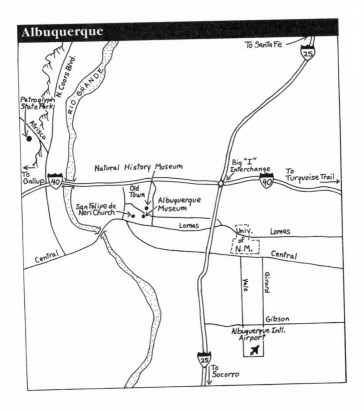

Albuquerque

spring, summer, and autumn months—sometimes free,
other times for a small admission fee; for the current
schedule of events, call 843-7270. The cultural center
also has a moderately priced restaurant specializing in
Native American cuisine, making it an ideal lunch stop.
Open daily from 9:00 a.m. to 5:30 p.m., closed Thanksgiving, Christmas, and New Year's Day. Admission to the
retail galleries is free; entry to the museum costs $2.50 for
adults, $1.50 for seniors over age 62, $1 for school-age
children. The center is at 2401 12th Street NW, a few
blocks north of I-40 exit 157B.

▲▲▲ **Sandia Crest**—A trip to the mountaintop is a must
for visitors, not only for the spectacular view but also
because temperatures on Sandia Crest average about 30

degrees cooler than downtown, offering a welcome escape from the city's midsummer afternoon heat. You can get to the summit by riding the world's longest aerial tramway or by driving the steep paved road up the back side of the mountain, a side trip from the Turquoise Trail.

To take the Sandia Peak Aerial Tramway (adults $10, seniors and students $7.50), go east on I-40 to Exit 167 and follow Tramway Boulevard north for 10 miles to the base terminal. The tramway operates daily during the summer months from 9:00 a.m. to 9:00 p.m., Friday and Saturday until 10:00 p.m., and during spring and autumn daily from 9:00 a.m. to 9:00 p.m. except Wednesday, when it does not begin running until 5:00 p.m.; closed during ski season.

To drive to the top of Sandia Crest and see the view for free, follow the Turquoise Trail (see Day 2). The steep, paved road up to Sandia Crest splits off to the left at Cedar Crest, the first town you reach on NM 14 after leaving the interstate.

An easy, mile-long walking trail along the crest between the tramway station and the auto road summit house gives you an eagle's-eye view of the city a mile below. There is a snack bar at the auto road summit house and a more complete restaurant and bar at the tramway station. The crest trail continues in both directions for a total distance of more than twenty miles.

Your itinerary for the next week lies before your eyes as you survey the 360-degree horizon from Sandia Crest. To the north, bordering the Rio Grande, the volcanic Jemez Mountains conceal Los Alamos and Bandelier National Monument (Day 3). The Sangre de Cristo Mountains to the northeast range from Santa Fe at the southern tip in a nearly unbroken wall of rock for 200 miles north past Taos into Colorado and beyond the Great Sand Dunes (Day 4). Far on the northern skyline, you may barely make out southwestern Colorado's San Juan Mountains, which you'll cross on your way west to Durango and Mesa Verde (Day 5). Then you'll return south through Chaco Canyon (Day 7) in the San Juan Basin, which lies between the Jemez Mountains and Mt. Taylor, the big solitary mountain that should be clearly visible to the west. South of Mt. Taylor are Ácoma, El Malpais, and El Morro (Days 21 and 22). Beyond Mt. Taylor is Navajo country.

"Sandia," by the way, means "watermelon" in Spanish.

▲▲ **Old Town**—Albuquerque's original town plaza, dating back to 1706, has remained remarkably intact as highrise buildings have sprouted up all around it in recent years, creating an oasis of antiquity in the midst of the modern city. Browse in the art galleries and shops; examine the wares of the Pueblo Indian vendors who line the sidewalks. Pause for a quiet moment in the eighteenth-century San Felipe de Neri Church on the northwest corner of the plaza. Free walking tours of Old Town start from the nearby Albuquerque Museum, 2000 Mountain Road NW, 243-7255, Wednesday through Friday at 11:00 a.m., Saturday and Sunday at 1:30 p.m. Old Town is one-half mile south of I-40 exit 157A via Rio Grande Boulevard.

▲ **Albuquerque's Museums**—You will have a chance to visit several of the Southwest's finest museums tomorrow in Santa Fe, but for serious museum buffs as well as visitors who find themselves in Albuquerque on an unlikely rainy day and want to do their sightseeing indoors, here is an array of first-rate possibilities:

The **New Mexico Museum of Natural History** contains full-scale dinosaur models, exhibits about New Mexico's human and animal inhabitants in the last Ice Age, and a large display about the Rio Grande including aquariums of fish that live in the river. The most unusual and memorable of the museum's exhibits is a quite realistic simulation of a journey into the depths of a volcano. Open daily from 10:00 a.m. to 5:00 p.m., adults $3, senior citizens $2, children ages 3 to 11 $1. The museum is at 1801 Mountain Road NW, near Old Town. For current exhibit information, call 841-8837.

The **Maxwell Museum of Anthropology** on the University of New Mexico campus contains exhibits on the Athabascan (Navajo and Apache) and Anasazi cultures, with special emphasis on Chaco Canyon, and provides a good introduction to many Native American tribes and sites you will see later in this itinerary. The university is about 2 miles east of I-25 via Central Avenue; Maxwell Museum is near the west edge of the campus, two blocks north of Central on Redondo Drive. Open Monday through Friday from 9:00 a.m. to 4:00 p.m., Saturday from 10:00 a.m. to 4:00 p.m., closed Sunday, free. Phone 277-4404 for information.

The **Spanish History Museum** displays the colonial history of New Mexico from the travels of early conquistadores to 1912, when statehood was granted. Other exhibits reveal the roles Hispanics have played in U.S. history, such as Spanish aid to George Washington's revolutionary army. The museum is two blocks south of the University of New Mexico at 2221 Lead SE. Open daily 1:00 to 5:00 p.m., donations welcome. Phone 268-9981 for information.

Camping

The most convenient public campground in the Albuquerque area is at **Coronado State Monument**, 15 minutes north of the city on I-25. Campsites, which cost $9, are along the Rio Grande riverbank. Pueblo ruins at the monument feature a kiva with rare restored wall murals.

Several private RV campgrounds with full hookups are located near I-40 at the western edge of the city. Try the **Albuquerque West KOA,** not far from Petroglyph Park, at 5739 Ouray Road NW one-half mile north of the Coors Road exit from I-40, 831-1991. Mesa-top campsites cost $15.

Lodging

For luxury accommodations in a historic hotel, Albuquerque's best is **La Posada de Albuquerque**, downtown at 125 Second Street (corner of Copper), (505) 242-9090, or, from outside New Mexico, (800) 621-7231. This was the first hotel ever built by New Mexico native Conrad Hilton. (It is no longer affiliated with the Hilton chain.) While the building only dates back to 1939, its lavish 1984 restoration has given it a distinctly Victorian air with classic New Mexican touches. Room rates range from $75 to $96 double.

Albuquerque has little to offer in the way of bed-and-breakfast inns, but one delightful exception is the **William E. Mauger Estate**, near Old Town at 701 Roma Avenue NW, (505) 242-8755. This three-story brick Queen Anne Victorian mansion, built in 1896, has eight guest rooms with antique furnishings and private baths. Room rates of $50 to $75 double include continental breakfast. Reservations are essential.

Name-brand motor hotels cluster around the intersection of I-25 and Lomas Boulevard, including the **Holiday Inn-Midtown**, 2020 Menaul Boulevard NE, (505) 884-2511, doubles $49 and up; **Howard Johnson's Midtown**, 900 Medical Arts Avenue NE, (505) 243-5693, doubles $53 and up; and the **Albuquerque Hilton**, 1901 University Boulevard NE, (505) 884-2500, doubles from $85. Farther north on I-25 is the **Holiday Inn Journal Center**, 5151 San Francisco Road NE (at exit 232), (505) 821-3333. Built in the shape of an Aztec pyramid, this hotel has a fifty-foot waterfall inside its ten-story atrium lobby. Rates are $78 to $98 double. Catering primarily to businessmen, several of these hotels offer special rates on weekend nights.

Good budget bets include the **Lorilodge Motel East** at 801 Central Avenue NE, just off I-25, (505) 243-2891, with doubles from $22 to $30, and the **De Anza Motel**, 4301 Central Avenue NE, (505)-255-1654, with doubles for under $30.

Food
The best bet for lunch is the restaurant at the **Indian Pueblo Cultural Center** (see Sightseeing Highlights),

open daily from 7:30 a.m. to 3:30 p.m. Specialties are Native American dishes such as Indian tacos, posole, and spiced bread pudding.

High on Sandia Crest, with prices to match, **High Finance** at the top of the tramway serves steaks, seafood, pasta, and Mexican food daily from 11:00 a.m. to 2:30 p.m. and 4:30 to 9:00 p.m., with barbecues on weekends. Sunset dining here makes for an incomparable experience. Guests with dinner reservations receive a discount on tram ticket prices.

Good places to dine around Old Town include **Antiquity**, 112 Romero NW, 247-3545, open Tuesday through Saturday from 5:00 to 10:00 p.m., and **High Noon**, 425 San Felipe NW, 765-1455, Monday through Saturday from 11:00 a.m. to 10:30 p.m. and Sunday from noon to 9:00 p.m., both fairly expensive and both specializing in Continental cuisine. For more moderate prices on Old Town Plaza, enjoy Mexican food at colorful **La Hacienda**, 243-3131, serving from 11:00 a.m. to 9:00 p.m. daily. A still more affordable restaurant in the same area, for lunch only, is **Christopher's**, 323 Romero NW, 242-0202, serving New Mexican food daily from 11:00 a.m. to 3:00 p.m.

For low-priced eating with the college crowd, especially recommended for breakfast, try the huevos rancheros (fried eggs on a tortilla, smothered in hot salsa) and giant cinnamon rolls at the **Frontier** on Central Avenue across from the University of New Mexico campus, open daily from 6:30 a.m. to midnight.

Hot Air Balloons

You can't go far in Albuquerque without seeing the ubiquitous hot air balloon motif that is this city's claim to fame. The **Albuquerque Balloon Fiesta**, held annually in early October, is the largest event of its kind in the world, featuring mass ascensions of over 500 balloons and drawing crowds of over half a million. If the Balloon Fiesta doesn't fit into your trip schedule, you can still see anywhere from a dozen to fifty balloons floating above the city, roaring with sounds like dragon breath and sometimes bouncing off suburban rooftops, practically any sunny weekend morning. The best spot from which to watch this spectacle is the rim of West Mesa Escarpment, reached via the maze of unpaved roads to the south above Petroglyph Park.

SANTA FE

From Albuquerque, a one-hour drive will take you across the stretch of rugged mountains and high desert to the gateway of one of our nation's most isolated corners, where history has created a tricultural blend that is unique in the world. Santa Fe has been New Mexico's capital since A.D. 1610.

Northern New Mexico feels foreign, and it's no wonder. For over two centuries, New Mexico was the northernmost Spanish colony in the New World, its border closed to foreigners. It became a state of newly independent Mexico in 1821 but was demoted to Mexican territorial status in 1836, invaded by the Republic of Texas in 1841, occupied by the U.S. Army in 1846 during the Mexican War, declared U.S. territory in 1848, and unsuccessfully invaded by the Confederacy in 1862. It became a U.S. state in 1912. Which nation owns New Mexico at the moment is of little import to local residents, who know their home is unlike anyplace else in America.

Suggested Schedule

9:00 a.m.	Drive the Turquoise Trail to Santa Fe.
10:30 a.m.	Stroll Santa Fe Plaza. See the Palace of the Governors, the New Mexico Fine Arts Museum, and art galleries.
1:00 p.m.	Green chile for lunch.
2:00 p.m.	Visit the Folk Art and Indian Arts museums or take an afternoon drive to Pecos.
Evening	Dinner and nightlife.

Travel Route: Albuquerque to Santa Fe (69 miles)
Drive the Turquoise Trail (NM 14) from Albuquerque to Santa Fe. It takes just 15 minutes longer than I-25 North and is a calmer, prettier drive. From the "Big I" (where I-40 intersects I-25) in Albuquerque, take I-40 East 15

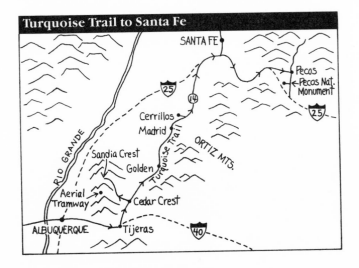

Turquoise Trail to Santa Fe

miles to exit 175 (Tijeras, Cedar Crest) and turn north (left) from the off-ramp.

The route takes you over the small but rugged Ortiz Range, site of the first gold discovery in what's now the United States. The former coal mining town of **Madrid**, once nearly abandoned and now revived by artists and refugees from modern living, has a mining museum with an underground tour, as well as one of the Santa Fe area's livelier live music night spots, the Mine Shaft Tavern.

Cerrillos, an off-the-beaten-path village with few concessions to tourism (or to the twentieth century) is worth a short stop and stroll. Follow the signs through town to the edge of the arroyo and visit Casa Grande, (505) 471-2744, an old 20-room adobe compound converted into a delightfully down-home bed and breakfast, petting zoo, and private museum of locally gathered turquoise, artifacts, and antique arroyo junk. If you have extra time, inquire at Casa Grande to arrange a personal four-wheel-drive and hiking tour of the old Pueblo Indian turquoise mines in the hills nearby.

When you reach I-25, don't continue into Santa Fe on NM 14 unless you're looking for a moderately priced

motel. The highway becomes Cerrillos Road, a congested
6-mile strip that is Santa Fe's "other side of the tracks."
Instead, take I-25 northbound for 6 miles to the Old
Pecos Trail exit for a more attractive approach to downtown Santa Fe.

Free Parking Downtown: When you cross the Santa
Fe River, you're within walking distance of the plaza.
Look for a parking spot along the river on Alameda
between Paseo de Peralta and Delgado Street. Walk one
long block north on Paseo de Peralta to Palace Avenue,
then three blocks east to the plaza. If you can't find parking on Alameda, turn around and follow Paseo de Peralta
north to the intersection with Washington Street (by the
big pink Moorish-style Masonic Temple) and turn right,
then right again onto Artist Road (follow the Hyde Park/
Ski Basin signs), and just above the Fort Marcy condo-
minium complex turn right again onto Prince Street. Park
anywhere along this street and walk across the mesa-top
park to the tall white Cross of the Martyrs for a view of
downtown, then descend the brick-cobbled walkway.
Walk 1½ blocks south (left) on Paseo de Peralta to Palace
Avenue and three blocks west (right) to the plaza.

Santa Fe

Santa Fe (pop. 60,000) prides itself on its antiquity and
blend of Native American, Hispanic, and Anglo cultural
influences. The Pueblo people have occupied the area for
at least 700 years, while the Hispanics arrived almost 400
years ago to establish the northernmost Spanish colony
in the New World. Santa Fe's population today is about 60
percent Hispanic, and a distinctive regional dialect of
Spanish is commonly spoken. The capital of a culturally
diverse state that also has Texas-style cattle ranching east
of the mountains, the Navajo Nation in the west, and the
Mexican border to the south, Santa Fe is a southwestern
microcosm.

Among Santa Fe's most noticeable characteristics is
adobe architecture. The Spanish Pueblo style, with pro-

Downtown Santa Fe

truding vigas (roof beams), is an adaptation of the Middle
Eastern architecture brought to Spain by the Moors and
to New Mexico by the Spanish, then influenced by
Pueblo Indian construction techniques. The territorial
style, with red bricks along the roofline, developed in the
late nineteenth century with the introduction of building
materials from the United States.

The city's Historic Styles Act, passed in 1957, requires
that all new construction in the downtown historic district be Spanish Pueblo or territorial in appearance, even
though modern building methods and materials may be
used. The law also limits building height and window

space and prohibits large or electrified signs. The result, a low-rise earth-tone city center preserving an Old World feel, is easy on the eyes.

Though museums and churches provide a framework for sightseeing, Santa Fe is a shopper's town, where Native American artifacts and traditional crafts, traditional western paintings, and contemporary Indian and non-Indian works of art, as well as aggressively regional Santa Fe-style "wearable art" fashions, are displayed in bewildering profusion. Quality is exceptional, with prices to match. Are you in the market for a painting that costs more than a car? If not, just browsing in the plaza area and Canyon Road galleries can introduce you to the visual glories of the American Southwest through the eyes of its best artists.

Santa Fe Downtown Walking Tour

One block east of the plaza or town square, on the north side of Palace Avenue, is Sena Plaza, a former Spanish colonial mansion whose interior courtyard provides a quiet, cool sitting spot. From there, proceed to the center of the plaza, where a monument commemorates Santa Feans' valor in repelling various nineteenth-century invaders such as Confederate troops and [   ] Indians. (The eradicated word was "savage." Locals hasten to point out that these weren't local Indians but rather Comanches who came from Texas—as, for that matter, did the Confederate soldiers.) Facing the plaza on the north side is the Palace of the Governors, housing the New Mexico Museum of History, a "must-see" for anyone interested in the region's Spanish colonial heritage. The next block west of the Palace is the New Mexico Fine Arts Museum. Allow at least two hours to see both museums.

When you exit the art museum, walk diagonally across the plaza to La Fonda, Santa Fe's oldest hotel. Browse through the hotel's lobby, interesting for its unusual decor, then exit and continue west up San Francisco Street to St. Francis Cathedral. Return from the cathedral to La Fonda and turn left (south) down Old Santa Fe Trail one block to Loretto Chapel on the grounds of the Inn at Loretto. On the same street, across the river, are San Miguel Mission and the Oldest House. Continue about two more blocks in the same direction on Old Santa Fe Trail to the New Mexico State Capitol Building, then backtrack to the plaza. At some point along this suggested tour, you'll probably be distracted by art galleries and shops. Wander and browse—you can't go wrong.

Santa Fe Sightseeing Highlights

▲▲▲ Palace of the Governors (New Mexico Museum of History)—This is the oldest public building in the United States, dating back to 1610. Emphasis is on the colonial and territorial eras. Permanent exhibits include photographic reproductions of Spanish colonial maps of the Southwest as well as a beautiful full-scale reconstruction of a Penitente chapel. Open daily from 10:00 a.m. to 5:00 p.m., closed Mondays off-season. Admission is $3 for adults, $1.25 for children ages 6 to 16. A two-day pass for admission to the Palace of the Governors, Fine Arts Museum, International Museum of Folk Art, and Museum of Indian Arts and Culture (in tomorrow's listings) costs only $5 and saves you $7 per person.

Indians selling jewelry and pottery at the Palace of the Governors portico enjoy official status as an "exhibit" of the Museum of New Mexico, which regulates the quality and authenticity of their goods.

▲▲▲ New Mexico Fine Arts Museum—Built in 1917 to encourage Santa Fe's burgeoning artist colony, the museum with its stylized neo-Spanish Pueblo look sparked a resurgence of the architecture that characterizes Santa Fe today. The museum formerly provided display space for local artists as well as a framing workshop in the basement and free monthly banquets upstairs. In those days, Santa Fe's artist population was small enough to fit in one room. Today the upstairs galleries house classic paintings from early-twentieth-century Santa Fe and Taos as well as work from The Studio, the 1930s forerunner of Santa Fe's Institute of American Indian Art. Notice the color technique in Navajo paintings displayed here, which resembles that of Walt Disney cartoons. Graduates of The Studio were hired by Disney for his first color animation features. The main floor galleries rotate exhibits with emphasis on contemporary New Mexican artists. St. Francis Auditorium, adjoining the museum, is patterned on a grand scale after the interiors of early New Mexican mission churches, with a series of frescoes depicting Franciscan missionary history. The museum is open daily from 10:00 a.m. to 5:00 p.m., closed Mondays off-season. Admission $3 for adults and $1.25 for children ages 6 to 16.

▲▲ St. Francis Cathedral—This church was built in 1869 by Archbishop Jean Baptiste Lamy, the French clergyman who was transferred here from Cleveland, Ohio, to restore mainstream Catholicism to New Mexico. (The Mexican government had banished all Spanish-born priests 41 years before. In isolation from the mother church, spiritual needs were served by the Brothers of Light, a lay Penitente sect that remains alive and well in rural New Mexico. After U.S. occupation, both the Catholic church and the federal government feared the Brotherhood's influence.) The cathedral's most notable feature is La Conquistadora, housed to the left of the altar in a chapel that was part of the original church on this site. The blue-clad willow wood statue of the Virgin, carried by Spanish refugees in their flight from the Pueblo Revolt of 1680, is the oldest surviving religious carving in New Mexico and the centerpiece of a thanksgiving procession (during Fiesta, the weekend after Labor Day) that has been held annually since 1716.

▲ Loretto Chapel (Chapel of Our Lady of Light)— Another Archbishop Lamy creation, the chapel is best known for its "miraculous staircase." Legend has it that the architect abandoned the project (some say he was caught with the bishop's nephew's wife) without building any stairs to the choir loft. A Mysterious Carpenter (the faithful believe he was St. Joseph, though skeptical historians claim he was an Austrian tourist) appeared and built this beautiful curved staircase without using any nails. Then he vanished without asking for payment. (Say, that *is* mysterious. . . .) Open daily from 9:00 a.m. to 5:00 p.m., admission 50 cents donation.

▲ **San Miguel Mission**—This chapel, claimed to be the Oldest Church in the United States, was built in 1710 on the rubble of a 1626 mission church destroyed during the Pueblo Revolt. Two other early mission churches still stand—at Ácoma (1629), which you'll see on Day 6, and at Isleta (1630)—so whether this one really counts as the oldest church is a matter of controversy. It's old, though, and reveals the spiritual side of Spanish colonial life. Indian relics are on display from the centuries-old pueblo that was demolished to build the earlier church. Open Monday through Saturday from 9:00 a.m. to 4:15 p.m. during the summer months, from 11:00 a.m. the rest of the year, and Sundays all year from 1:00 to 4:15 p.m. Donations are accepted. There is a Catholic curio shop.

▲ **Oldest House**—Next door to San Miguel Mission, this isn't really the oldest house in the United States (several houses at Ácoma Pueblo in New Mexico and the Hopi village of Oraibi in Arizona, which you'll visit later in this tour, date back more than 800 years). Barrio de Analco, of which this house is a part, quartered Indian laborers brought from Mexico in the seventeenth century. Here you'll get an idea of everyday living conditions in colonial New Mexico.

▲ **State Capitol**—A big circular flat-roofed neoterritorial style building, the "Roundhouse" looks nothing like a capitol building is supposed to. Its floor plan was patterned after the Zia Pueblo sun symbol that graces the New Mexico flag and license plates. Stroll through the gardens, landscaped with vegetation from all parts of New Mexico, and the rotunda. A former state capitol, still the prettiest building in the state government complex, is the nearby Bataan Building, whose classic dome was removed in 1951. Open Monday through Friday from 8:00 a.m. to 5:00 p.m. and on Saturdays during the summer months from 9:00 a.m. to 4:00 p.m.

▲▲ **Canyon Road**—Drive up Canyon Road, the first left turn off Paseo de Peralta after you cross the river heading south, to see the original center of Santa Fe's artist colony, now a mixed bag of small studio/galleries and more commercial restaurants and shops. If Santa Fe's art scene has sparked an urge in you to take up sketching again (you'll find plenty of inspiration in the coming weeks), the Artisan on Canyon Road is among the most complete art supply stores you're ever likely to find.

Where Canyon Road stops being one way, turn right on Camino del Monte Sol and drive south to Old Santa Fe Trail. Take a one-block jog to your right (downhill) to Camino Lejo, with its big "Museums" sign, and turn there to find the following three museums where you can spend the whole morning and wish you had more time.

▲▲ **New Mexico Museum of Indian Arts and Culture** —This outstanding museum presents selections from the state of New Mexico's 50,000 Indian artifacts, with Native American participation in exhibit planning, and works from the Institute of American Indian Art. One exhibit shows aerial photographs of Pueblo ruins that non-Indians cannot visit in person, including the ancient pueblo on Black Mesa above San Ildefonso Pueblo (Day 3). There are often craft demonstrations. The gift shop has an excellent selection of books on Indian subjects. Open daily from 10:00 a.m. to 5:00 p.m., closed Mondays off-season; admission $3 for adults, $1.25 for children ages 6 to 16.

▲▲▲ **New Mexico Museum of International Folk Art**—Among the most unusual museums anywhere, this is the place in Santa Fe to take children if you have any along. It can also bring out the childlike wonder in you. Amble through the Spanish colonial and other folk art exhibits to the Girard Wing, where you'll find a phenomenal collection of handcrafted toys and miniatures from throughout the world arranged in enchanting dioramas. The museum's gift shop is wonderful. Open daily from 10:00 a.m. to 5:00 p.m., closed Mondays off-season. Admission is $3 for adults, $1.25 for children ages 6 to 16.

▲▲▲ **Wheelwright Museum of American Indian Art**—This small private museum features rotating traditional and modern Native American art exhibits. It was founded, with guidance from famed Navajo shaman Hosteen Klah, by Mary Wheelwright, daughter of an aristocratic Bostonian family who came west to live among the Indians. The building is in the eight-sided hogan shape that Navajo ceremonies require. Downstairs, Case Trading Post sells Native American arts and crafts of assured quality in all price ranges as well as books, posters, and handmade cards. Open daily from 9:00 a.m. to 5:00 p.m., donations welcome.

▲ **Randall Davey Audubon Center**—If you'd rather be outdoors, make time in your morning schedule to visit the estate of a longtime Santa Fe artist who left his home and 135-acre grounds to the National Audubon Society as a wildlife refuge. At the mouth of Santa Fe Canyon (a municipal watershed that has been closed to the public for 50 years), wildlife that sometimes wanders down to these meadows includes coyotes, raccoons, black bears, mountain lions, bobcats, and mule deer. The refuge is home to over 100 species of birds and 120 species of plants. The grounds are open daily from 9:00 a.m: to 5:00 p.m. A $1 admission fee is requested from non-Audubon members. Call (505) 983-4609 for information on guided history tours of the Randall Davey house.

To get there, take Canyon Road as far as it goes. When it seems to end, jog one block to the right, then left onto Upper Canyon Road. The Randall Davey Center is as far up Upper Canyon Road as you're allowed to drive.

▲ **Institute of American Indian Arts**—Operated by the federal government, IAIA provides free training for the most talented young Indian artists from all over the United States. Its presence has been a major factor in the emergence of Santa Fe as the largest market for contemporary Native American art. The museum at the school provides space for frequently changing exhibitions of student work as well as pieces donated by alumni. Presently located at 1369 Cerrillos Road about 2 miles south-

west of downtown, the museum is open Monday through
Friday from 9:00 a.m. to 5:00 p.m. Admission is free. At
the time of this revision, a bill is pending in the U.S. Congress which would enable the museum to move into
more spacious quarters downtown in the now-empty old
Federal Building across the street from St. Francis
Cathedral.

Camping
A good camping area near Santa Fe is the National Forest
Black Canyon Campground ($5 sites) or adjoining
Hyde Memorial State Park ($6 sites), both 7 miles up
Hyde Park-Ski Basin Road from downtown (take Washington Street north from downtown and turn right at the
sign). If you decide to stay in town late for nightlife and
after-hours window-shopping, camping spots will still be
available at Hyde Park, a popular picnic area where sites
are often occupied until late in the afternoon by day
users. Overnight parking is also allowed 10 miles farther
up the road at the Ski Basin parking area, a major Pecos
Wilderness trailhead with picnic tables and rest rooms.
    Hyde Park is nearly 9,000 feet in altitude, compared
with 5,000 feet in Albuquerque and 7,000 feet in Santa Fe.
The Ski Basin parking lot is over 10,000 feet, about the
same as the summit of Sandia Crest. As you probably
noticed this morning on Sandia, higher elevations mean
cooler temperatures. Each 1,000 feet of altitude drops the
temperature about 9 degrees F, as great a difference as
traveling 300 miles north, so temperatures at Hyde Park
average 35 degrees cooler than in Albuquerque, about the
same as in Calgary, Alberta. Nights can be chilly at any
time of year. By the way, the vehicles-prohibited maintenance road that runs 6 miles up to the 12,010-foot summit of Lake Peak from the Aspen Vista parking area midway between Hyde Park and the Ski Basin makes for
lovely walking. In early October it becomes a "must-see"
sight, as autumn colors brighten the largest continuous
forest of aspen trees in the world.
    Apache Canyon KOA is a large commercial camp-

ground with full hookups located on Old Pecos Trail, the two-lane highway that parallels I-25 northbound from Santa Fe. Sites cost about $12. Another campground within easy driving distance of Santa Fe is operated by Indians. The **Tesuque Pueblo RV Campground** is just off US 285 next to the landmark Camel Rock, 10 miles north of the city. Amenities include a heated swimming pool, a hot tub, and a bingo parlor just across the highway. Nearby Tesuque Pueblo is small but picturesque. Sites cost about $12.

Lodging

Choosing to stay in town rather than camping tonight will give you a better chance to enjoy evening entertainment. Most downtown hotels are luxurious and costly, starting at just under $100 double. Within walking distance of the plaza, try **La Fonda**, 100 E. San Francisco, (505) 982-5511, Santa Fe's oldest hotel and still one of the best; **Hotel St. Francis**, 210 Don Gaspar, (505) 983-5700, newly renovated as an elegant small hotel; or **La Posada de Santa Fe**, 330 E. Palace, (505) 983-6351, formerly a Victorian mansion.

Santa Fe has several bed-and-breakfast inns. Since a city ordinance restricts B&Bs to areas with commercial zoning, most are within easy walking distance of the plaza. My favorite, because its small size (just four guest rooms) makes for an exceptionally homelike atmosphere, is the new **Inn of the Animal Tracks**, 707 Paseo de Peralta, (505) 988-1546. Innkeeper Daun Martin formerly managed the famous Britt House in San Diego and is as close to a perfect hostess as you'll ever meet. Her love for animals pervades the house (each guest bedroom has a different animal theme), but since she keeps pets on the premises, guests cannot bring theirs. The $80 room rate includes a full breakfast as well as afternoon tea and dessert—the best homemade pies in town. For more formal bed-and-breakfast accommodations, go to the **Grant Corner Inn**, 122 Grant, (505) 983-6678, a turn-of-the-century brick mansion across from the Safeway super-

market a block west and a block north of the Fine Arts
Museum, where rates range from $60 to $100 double, full
breakfast included. Approximately a dozen other Santa Fe
bed and breakfasts can be booked through Santa Fe Central Reservations, (505) 983-8200 or (800) 982-7669 outside of New Mexico.

You'll find several lower-cost motels along busy Cerrillos Road, which runs for miles diagonally southwest
from downtown. The best rates close to downtown are at
the **Santa Fe Travelodge**, 646 Cerrillos Road, (505)
982-3551, where doubles start under $50.

Warning: Santa Fe accommodations tend to fill up
quickly on Wednesday through Saturday nights during
Opera season, mid-July through mid-August, so if you
are traveling without reservations, check into your hotel
or motel as soon as you arrive in town, before sightseeing
or eating. Another warning: for Indian Market weekend,
the third weekend in August, all accommodations in the
Santa Fe area are booked up as much as four months in
advance, and it may be impossible to find lodging on
short notice even in Albuquerque or Los Alamos!

Food

Green chile is what distinguishes New Mexican cuisine
from any other. New Mexicans grow more chile peppers
than the rest of the United States combined and prefer to
eat them as a roasted, peeled, and usually diced vegeta-
ble, by the bowlful or poured over practically anything.
The quality of chile is judged by how "hot" it is, so
restaurants compete to bring tears of ecstasy to their
patrons' eyes. When a waitress asks, "Red or green?"
don't make the common error of assuming that green
must be milder than red. The green chile at any self-
respecting Santa Fe restaurant will knock your socks off.

For regional cuisine in Santa Fe, there are myriad possibilities. **Tomasita's**, 500 S. Guadalupe, (505) 983-5721,
has good New Mexican lunches and dinners, including
daily specials, at moderate prices. **The Burrito Company**, just off the plaza on Washington Street, serves Mex-

ican fast food smothered in green chile and has a sidewalk patio perfect for people-watching. **Tia Sophia's**, 210 W. San Francisco, is an unpretentious coffee shop for breakfast or lunch. The spicy food here is guaranteed to wake you up!

Santa Fe has about 200 restaurants, constantly changing, serving everything from Greek grape leaves to green chile tempura. Pick up a current restaurant guide from the La Fonda tourist information desk for an array of possibilities. When stocking up on picnic supplies, be sure to pick up a loaf or two of the delicious homemade bread, baked in horno ovens, that Indian vendors sell on the streets around the plaza. The only way to take green chile back home is in the form of jelly, jam, or relish, available in many gift shops. Other great edible souvenirs are piñon nuts, red chile ristras, and Indian blue corn. Blue corn tortilla chips are sold in Santa Fe supermarkets. Blue cornmeal can be boiled into a tasty hot cereal called atole, similar to cream of wheat, or substituted in any recipe that uses cornmeal (use buttermilk instead of regular milk for a brighter blue color). Pueblo Indians, who hold blue corn sacred, make it into a crisp paper-thin bread called piki for festivals and religious ceremonies.

Nightlife

From the moment you leave Santa Fe until you reach Las Vegas two weeks from now, evening entertainment will consist of crackling campfires, spectacularly starry skies, and an occasional ranger slide show. If you want to get out and boogie, tonight's the night.

The larger downtown hotels all have lounges, piano bars, or the like. For quiet, cozy elegance, stop in at the **Staab House** bar in La Posada, east of Paseo de Peralta on Palace Avenue, with its authentic Victorian era furnishings and notorious resident ghost. Ask anyone who works there about her.

Club West, on Alameda at the southwest edge of downtown, lures a widely mixed audience with an eclectic assortment of high-energy live music. Tonight it might be rock 'n roll, African pop, Texas blues, or salsa music; or it could be the only chance you'll ever have to see Indians dance to a reggae beat. Cover charge varies; music starts at 9:30 p.m. nightly. A good place to meet Santa Fe locals is **El Farol** on Canyon Road at Palace Avenue, a friendly neighborhood bar in a uncommon neighborhood. Folk musicians perform some nights for a small cover. There are rarely any open tables after 9:00 p.m. Join a group of strangers and you'll find yourself welcome. It's that kind of place.

Santa Fe's summer calendar is packed with cultural performances and spectator events. The most famous is the **Santa Fe Opera**, on US 285 3 miles north of town, mid-July through mid-August. Tickets are expensive and hard to get on short notice, but if you dress as elegantly as possible (wearing blue jeans to the opera is considered déclassé, though many locals used to and some still do) and ask at the box office, your chances of getting inexpensive standing-room tickets and finding vacant seats later are good. Call 982-3855 for information.

For something completely different in the way of theater entertainment, consider the **Madrid Melodrama**, held during the summer months in the town of Madrid, which you went through on the Turquoise Trail this morning. Melodramas for tourists can be found throughout the west in the summer, but this one is the most authentic I've ever witnessed, with its straight-faced presentations of genuine Victorian plays in an old railroad barn that recalls the kinds of places where touring companies actually performed in small towns a century ago. The playhouse even has a real locomotive, adding realism when the script calls for a heroine to be tied to the railroad tracks. Bring a bag of marshmallows and learn first-hand why they came to be known as "villain bullets." Tickets cost $6.50. Call 473-0743 for current performance information.

Other events range from the **Santa Fe Chamber Music Festival** to the **Rodeo de Santa Fe**. Check the weekly (Thursday to Wednesday) *Reporter* or the *New*

Mexican's Friday "Pasatiempo" supplement for complete entertainment listings and reviews.

Itinerary Option: Pecos

For a pleasant afternoon outdoors, drive about 20 miles east (northbound) from Santa Fe on I-25 to the second Pecos exit and visit Pecos National Monument, the site of a major pueblo ruin that dates back to the thirteenth century A.D. and a Spanish mission from the seventeenth century. The Pecos pueblo was the eastern gateway to the Rio Grande pueblo country, and it prospered through trade. A long, massive wall, still partly standing, separated the pueblo from the camping area for visiting groups of Indians from the eastern plains. The pueblo was abandoned in the mid-1800s after Comanche raids wiped out much of the population, and the survivors' descendants now live at Jemez Pueblo in the mountains north of Albuquerque.

After visiting the national monument, you may wish to continue west through the village and enjoy a scenic 20-mile drive up the Pecos River Canyon, a popular trout fishing area with enclaves of vacation cabins. The pavement ends at the Terrero General Store, and from there an unpaved road that can be quite rough and hard on vehicles leads to a series of free campgrounds and trailheads at the edge of the Pecos Wilderness. Midway up the paved portion of the road, a dirt road turns off into Dalton Canyon, used as a hideout by the notorious outlaw Dalton Gang for many years in the late nineteenth century. The canyon is a pretty spot for walking and picnicking.

BANDELIER NATIONAL MONUMENT AND LOS ALAMOS

Los Alamos, White Rock, and Bandelier National Monument occupy parts of the Pajarito Plateau, a ledge of lava and ash formed by a huge volcano. If you could view the area from above, you would see that the mountain range to the west is actually circular, the crumbled remains of the rim of the volcano, which some geologists believe stood higher than Mount Everest some 1,700,000 years ago. The entire area has been nominated for national park status three times—first in 1919 and most recently in 1986. While all three attempts have been blocked by the forest products industry, nobody has ever doubted that the area's scenic beauty and unique features rival those of the Grand Canyon, Yosemite, or Yellowstone. Here, side by side, you'll find pre-Columbian Indian ruins and the birthplace of the nuclear age.

The area is a one-hour drive from Santa Fe. Along the way you can visit an outdoor sculpture gallery and a modern Indian pueblo.

Suggested Schedule

8:00 a.m.	Breakfast.
9:00 a.m.	Drive to Bandelier National Monument, visiting Shidoni's sculpture gardens and San Ildefonso Pueblo en route.
11:00 a.m.	Arrive at Bandelier. Explore the Indian ruins and enjoy a picnic lunch.
2:00 p.m.	Stay in Bandelier for an afternoon of hiking or explore the Los Alamos area.
5:00 p.m.	Take your choice: return to Santa Fe, camp in Bandelier, or spend the night in Los Alamos or White Rock.

Travel Route: Santa Fe to Bandelier National Monument (40 miles)

Leave Santa Fe on Bishop's Lodge Road and drive 5 miles to Tesuque, stopping at Shidoni Art Foundry (watch for it on your left) to walk around acres of parklike outdoor sculpture gallery. If you own a skyscraper or shopping mall and want a really large piece of art to put in front of it, here's where you can buy one.

Join US 285 northbound at Tesuque for 9 miles to the Los Alamos-Bandelier exit on the left, and follow NM 502 west.

After about 5 miles, you'll see the turnoff on the right to San Ildefonso Pueblo. In another 3 miles, you'll cross the Rio Grande. (Bandelier, your destination, is just 17 miles from Santa Fe as the crow flies, but you have to drive more than twice that distance because this is the only bridge over the river.) The road divides 4 miles past the river, one fork going to Los Alamos and the other to White Rock and Bandelier.

Leaving Bandelier, if you turn left from the entrance instead of backtracking to the right, you will reach a shortcut to Los Alamos in a few miles. This road takes you past Pajarito Canyon, one of the Pajarito Plateau sightseeing highlights mentioned below. When you pass the Los Alamos National Laboratories administration buildings, where the Bradbury Science Museum is located, turn left at the stoplight, cross the bridge, and then turn right on Trinity Drive to reach the Los Alamos central business district. Jog one block north at the first opportunity to reach the historical museum and Fuller Lodge Art Gallery.

Leaving Los Alamos, Trinity Drive will put you back on NM 502 for a spectacular descent along the canyon wall.

Sightseeing Highlights
▲ **San Ildefonso Pueblo**—While the most striking Indian pueblos in New Mexico, Taos (Day 4) and Ácoma (Day 21), seem like fragments of the past, San Ildefonso typifies modern-day pueblos along the Rio Grande. The central plaza is much larger than those at most other pueblos; San Ildefonso has two separate kiva clans, so during ceremonies two dances are often held simultaneously on opposite sides of the plaza. The mission-style

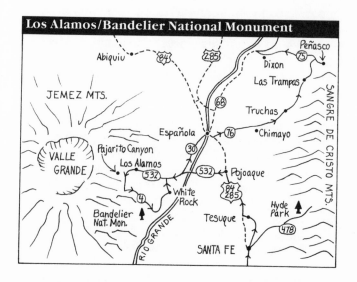

Los Alamos/Bandelier National Monument

church was built around 1970 to replace an old one. Behind the pueblo rises a massive volcanic rock formation called Black Mesa. A sacred spot to the San Ildefonso people, whose ancestors retreated to live on top of it when the Spanish returned after the Pueblo Revolt of 1680, the mesa is forbidden to non-Indians.

The distinctive rakulike black pottery style developed at San Ildefonso by the late Maria Martinez (a film about her is shown at national parks and monuments throughout the Four Corners area) is prized by collectors and found in museums around the world. A collection of Maria's pottery can be seen upon request at the Popovi Da Studio in the pueblo, open daily during the summer months from 10:00 a.m. to 5:00 p.m., closed weekends and Wednesdays during May and October. Arts and crafts are more important than ever to this pueblo. The exceptionally large plaza makes San Ildefonso the perfect site for the annual Eight Northern Pueblos Artist and Craftsman Show. A relatively small event until recently, this show held on a weekend in mid-July (call the pueblo at 455-2273 for dates) has grown to rival the Santa Fe Indian

Market with 400 exhibitors from around the nation. It is
the only Indian arts and crafts show in New Mexico that
is owned and operated by Indians. The pueblo also has a
small museum, open during the summer on weekdays
only from 8:00 a.m. to 5:00 p.m.

▲▲▲ **Bandelier National Monument**—The birthplace
of southwestern archaeology, now a hikers' paradise, is
named for Adolph Bandelier, a Swiss immigrant and self-
taught Native American scholar. In 1880, he was the first
southwestern archaeologist to excavate and study Indian
ruins instead of looting them for collectible artifacts.
Unexcavated pueblo ruins, found throughout the Jemez
Mountains, are crumbled, buried, hard to recognize, not
much to look at. Bandelier's excavation was the proto-
type for restoring all the Anasazi ruins that are visitor
attractions today.

The ruins behind the visitors center stand as the crown-
ing achievement of Bandelier's thirty-four years of work.
The settlement dates from the postclassical Pueblo period
(A.D. 1400, after the decline of the Chaco culture, of
which you'll see more in a few days).

Only a stone floor plan remains of what was once a
three-story castlelike walled town, while nearby cliff
dwellings are better preserved. Climb to the Ceremonial
Cave for the best view of the ruins and their magnificent
canyon setting.

The road takes you in only to the corner of the monument; beyond the visitors center and ruins is a large, rugged hikers-only wilderness area. A round-trip hike to the
far boundary would take three full days. For an enjoyable
day hike, explore more of Frijoles Canyon. The **Falls
Trail**, downstream from the end of the backpackers'
parking area across the bridge from the visitors center, is
a 1½-mile (one-way) hike that packs cool creekside forests, cliffs, volcanic tent rocks, and a lovely waterfall view
into a challenging 2½-hour hike. For a longer, all-afternoon
or even all-day excursion, get a free wilderness permit
from the visitors center and hike the **Upper Frijoles
Trail**, rock-hopping and sometimes splashing back and

forth across the creek. Watch for golden eagles, turkey vultures, and red-tailed hawks overhead. Go as far as you like; the trail continues about 8 miles to the upper end of Frijoles Canyon. (This is a more enjoyable day hike than the more popular Stone Lions Trail, a hot trip that's much more strenuous than it appears on the map because midway it traverses Alamo Canyon, both deeper and steeper than Frijoles Canyon.)

Admission to the national monument is $5 per vehicle. Instead, you may want to buy a Golden Eagle Pass, good for free admission to all national parks and monuments for the rest of the calendar year. The cash savings from using the pass on this trip will be significant. It will encourage you to visit less-known U.S. fee areas you might otherwise skip, and flashing your pass at the entrance will make you feel like a VIP.

▲▲ **Los Alamos**—The hidden site of the ultimate Top Secret Government Project during World War II is now a cozy all-American community with incomparable views. People here work at the nuclear research laboratory, so big you can't miss it. (You can't go in, either.) To learn more about high technology and/or the birth of the bomb, visit the outstanding **Bradbury Science Museum**, where you'll see mementos of the Manhattan Project, hands-on computer and laser exhibits, an antique atomic bomb, and explanations of other technologies developed at the labs which are difficult to pronounce, let alone comprehend. Open Tuesday through Friday from 9:00 a.m. to 5:00 p.m., Saturday through Monday 1:00 to 5:00 p.m., the museum is located next to the LANL administration building near the stoplight across the Los Alamos Canyon bridge from downtown. Admission is free.

The **Los Alamos County Historical Museum** and **Fuller Lodge Art Center** occupy buildings of the pre-World War II Los Alamos Ranch School, where children from wealthy eastern families were sent to get healthy through outdoor living. The historical museum tells about the joys and rigors of life at the ranch school, as well as the war years at Los Alamos. Fuller Lodge Art Center provides exhibition space for a community cooperative of local artists, a refreshing contrast to Santa Fe's big-money art market. Near the corner of Central Avenue and 20th Street, both museums are open Monday through Saturday from 10:00 a.m. to 4:00 p.m., Sunday 1:00 to 4:00 p.m. There is a small pueblo ruin in the park behind the lodge.

▲ **Pajarito Plateau and Valle Grande**—If Congress were to create Pajarito National Park or Jemez National Park (the names that have actually been proposed), the following little-known spots would be a few of the points of interest:

White Rock Overlook—As you drive into the Los Alamos bedroom community of White Rock on your way to Bandelier National Monument, turn left on Rover Drive and follow the signs to White Rock Overlook in a municipal park on the tip of the mesa. Seven hundred feet below runs a seemingly untouched wild stretch of the Rio Grande. To the north, Black Mesa looms at the end of the canyon, and beyond it you can see the rugged Sangre de Cristo Mountains running all the way up into Colorado. Behind you, a thin waterfall plunges into a side canyon. The only way to reach the river below is by a steep trail that descends to the canyon bottom in less than a mile. You can see the trail toward your right from the overlook, but finding its starting point is trickier. The trailhead, well hidden near the picnic ground about a hundred yards to the right of the overlook, is marked only by two old fence posts on the rim.

Pajarito Canyon—Follow NM 503, the paved road that goes west (uphill, toward the mountains) from the stoplight near the LANL administration building and the science museum. The road curves around to the south and passes a paved side road on the right that goes to the Los Alamos ski area. Continue on NM 503 for about half a mile and watch for the next road on the right, an unpaved, unmarked forest road that runs in both directions parallel to the main road. Park beside this road and follow the dirt road north (downhill); it curves to the west, following a small creek, and ends after a quarter of a mile, but a trail continues up Pajarito Canyon from here. What distinguishes this from all the other dozen or so canyons in the area is the narrow passageway between the rock walls which prevented timber from being cut in the canyon. This is the only untouched old growth forest in the Jemez Mountains, lush and magnificent. Locals refer to it as "the rain forest." Black bears are sometimes spotted farther back in the canyon.

Valle Grande—Continuing on NM 503 west for about 10 steep miles beyond the entrance to Bandelier National Monument, you will reach the upper rim of the Jemez Mountains and soon see Valle Grande, which is said to be the world's largest volcano caldera, with a smaller, more recent volcano cone in its center. It would look very much like Crater Lake in Oregon, except that a narrow canyon on the far side lets the water run out. Is the volcano extinct? Consider the fact that dozens of hot springs exist throughout the area. On the west side of the caldera, Los Alamos National Laboratories maintains a geothermal pilot project to experiment with ways to convert the earth's heat to useful energy. Something is causing all that heat so close beneath the surface. Extinct? Don't bet on it.

Cliff Dwellings—There are over ten thousand known archaeological sites on the Pajarito Plateau. If you look closely, you can see the remnants of cliff dwellings on the south-facing side of every canyon, most easily spotted by the man-made holes that once held roof supports. In fact, around A.D. 1400, more people lived in this area than are here today. If you watch along the sides of any highway in the Los Alamos area, you will see locked gates that often have two white signs lettered too small to read and a walkway at the side of the gate. The signs do not say "Keep out." One says that camping, hunting, and certain other activities are prohibited; the other warns that it is against the law to remove Indian artifacts—a good indication that Indian ruins are there. As long as the area is not posted with "No trespassing" signs, you are free to enter and explore. (If there are "No trespassing" signs, heed them absolutely. Remember that back in the 1940s they were very casual about disposing of nuclear waste, and a few areas around Los Alamos are permanently radioactive!)

Camping

Bandelier's mesa-top campground has an easy trail to the canyon rim for evening walks as well as nightly campfire talks and running water. Camping costs $5 plus admission to the national monument. There are no hookups.

Lodging

The nearest motel to Bandelier is the **White Rock Motor Lodge**, (505) 672-3838, 10 miles northeast of the monument entrance on NM Loop 4 in the town of White Rock. Some rooms have kitchenettes, and all have satellite TV. Rooms cost $47 per night double. Los Alamos has two motels—the **Hilltop House** at Trinity and Central, (505) 662-2441, with rooms starting at $56 per night, and the **Los Alamos Inn**, 2201 Trinity, (505)-662-7211, with rooms starting at $48 double.

Food

In Bandelier National Monument, a small snack bar adjoins the gift shop near the visitors center.

White Rock has five restaurants, all moderately priced. Try **Cheers Family Restaurant**, 672-3661, for soup, sandwiches, Mexican food, and breakfast served all day, open Monday 9:30 a.m. to 8:00 p.m., Tuesday through Saturday 6:30 a.m. to 9:00 p.m., and Sunday 7:00 a.m. to 3:00 p.m. In Los Alamos, **Colores Restaurant** at 820 Trinity, 662-6285, serves New Mexican food for lunch (weekdays only) from 11:00 a.m. to 3:00 p.m. and dinner from 5:00 to 8:00 p.m. **Boccaccio's**, on the golf course at 4244 Diamond Drive, 662-7204, features steaks, seafood, and pasta for lunch (weekdays only) from 11:30 a.m. to 2:00 p.m. and dinner (Tuesday through Saturday) from 5:30 to 8:30 p.m., Friday until 9:00 p.m.

TAOS AND THE GREAT SAND DUNES

This will be the first full driving day of your trip, with an intermission in Taos. The High Road to Taos takes you through old Spanish colonial villages and into Carson National Forest, then descends to Rio Grande State Park. In the Taos area, visit Taos Pueblo and perhaps D. H. Lawrence's ranch. Later in the afternoon, drive north to Great Sand Dunes National Monument. Hike the dunes.

Suggested Schedule

8:30 a.m.	Break camp. Drive to Española, Chimayo, and the High Road to Taos, stopping at Picuris Pueblo and then descending through Dixon.
11:00 a.m.	Drive through Rio Grande State Park to Taos.
12:00 noon	Lunch, see Taos.
1:30 p.m.	Visit Taos Pueblo.
2:30 p.m.	Stop at D. H. Lawrence Ranch or Millicent Rogers Museum.
3:30 p.m.	Drive to Great Sand Dunes.
5:30 p.m.	Camp at Great Sand Dunes or take a motel in Alamosa.

Travel Route: Los Alamos to Taos (99 miles)

From Los Alamos, White Rock, or Bandelier, descend the Pajarito Plateau on NM 502 and, before reaching the Rio Grande, turn left on the paved back road to Española, which parallels the river and takes you past Black Mesa and Santa Clara Pueblo. The road to Puye Cliff Dwellings turns off to the west midway along this road. The cliff dwellings, the ancestral home of the Santa Clara people since the twelfth century A.D., extend in several levels for about 2 miles along the face of the cliff. You can see the cliff dwellings at a distance before deciding whether to pay the $4 per person admission charge, which goes to Santa Clara Pueblo. There is also a large pueblo ruin on top of the mesa, partially restored and still used for ceremonies by residents of the modern pueblo.

From Española, turn right and drive through town to find NM 76 east to Chimayo, 10 miles into the foothills of the Sangre de Cristo range. As you approach Chimayo, watch for the sign to "Santuario" and follow it. **Santuario de Chimayo**, a small twin-towered church built entirely without nails in 1816, is believed by northern New Mexico's Catholics to be a place of miracles—the Lourdes of the American frontier. In a small room through another room to the left of the altar is El Pozito ("the little well"), where for over two centuries the faithful have taken pinches of clay for its healing properties. The crutches and braces in the adjoining room have been left as testimony that it works. Between Good Friday and Easter, thousands of people from throughout northern New Mexico line the roads, some carrying crosses, in pilgrimage to Chimayo.

Return to NM 76 and continue north up and down the hills. This is the most picturesque segment of the High Road to Taos. Each valley has a small village of farmers and woodcutters which dates back to Spanish colonial times. At the base of 13,102-foot Truchas Peak, **Truchas** (the name means "trout") was used in 1986 as the filming location for *The Milagro Beanfield War*, directed by Robert Redford from New Mexico author John Nichols's novel. Just off the highway at **Las Trampas** ("the traps") is an imposing mission church that dates back to 1751.

At **Picuris (San Lorenzo) Pueblo**, near the village of Peñasco, NM 76 ends in a T-intersection with NM 75. Secluded in its mountain valley, Picuris Pueblo has a restaurant, a fishing lake, and a small museum, where you can see examples of the unusual micaceous pottery that has been made here for 800 years. Mica in the local clay gives the pots an iridescent, almost bronzelike appearance. This pottery has recently become popular among Indian pottery collectors. While most residents of Picuris Pueblo live in government project housing, the ancient pueblo is being restored, and tours are available for a small fee.

Northern New Mexico

From the highway intersection at Picuris, following the signs to Taos—turning right and then, 7 miles later, left on NM 3 through Carson National Forest—is the shorter (26 miles) but not much faster route. I suggest, instead, that you turn left (west) on NM 75, which will take you down a continuous 17-mile descent to the Rio Grande, passing through the artists-and-apple-orchards community of **Dixon**. When you return to US 285/NM 68, turn right (north) and go 10 miles to Pilar. Turn right, following the sign to **Rio Grande Gorge State Park**. A $2 day-use fee is charged for picnicking in the park but not for driving through. The road follows the riverbank up the gorge, past several picnic areas. When the pavement ends, turn right (east). The road climbs out of the canyon, affording a good view of the Taos Valley with Wheeler Peak (at 13,161 feet, the highest mountain in New Mexico) in the background. Soon the pavement resumes and zips you into downtown Taos.

Taos

The northernmost outpost of Spanish colonial America, founded five years after Santa Fe, Taos was the third permanent European settlement in what's now the United States. It was a major center for trade with people who weren't allowed farther into Spanish territory—the Navajo, Ute, and plains tribes as well as French and Anglo mountain men.

In 1898, two American artists, Bert Phillips and Ernest Blumenschein, were bound for Mexico on a sketching expedition but made it only as far as Taos before their wagon broke down. Enchanted by the land, the exotic people, and the strangely vivid quality of the light, they stayed to form the nucleus of Taos' active artist community. Other artists came to Taos from Europe at the outbreak of World War I, and beginning in the 1920s, the town's cultural scene enjoyed international renown as the "Left Bank" of the American frontier.

Taos depends almost entirely on tourism and the arts (perhaps a natural continuation of the town's historic role—trading with "barbarians" from the north). With its beautiful natural setting and rich tricultural heritage, it may be among the best places in the world to live if you don't need a job. The largest employer in Taos County is the Highway Department.

Entering Taos along three congested miles of strip city,

you'll go up a block-long hill as you enter the historic district. Turn left at the top of the hill to the pretty, modernized town plaza.

Taos Sightseeing Highlights

▲ **Kit Carson Home and Museum**—On Kit Carson Road (Highway 64) just across the main highway from the plaza area, this 12-room adobe was Kit Carson's home for 25 years from 1843 to 1868. It houses a museum of territorial period antiques and a small chapel. Open daily from 8:00 a.m. to 6:00 p.m. during the summer months, 9:00 a.m. to 5:00 p.m. the rest of the year; admission $2.50 for adults, $2 for senior citizens, $1.50 for children ages 6 to 15. Kit Carson's grave is two blocks to the north in the park named after him.

▲ **Blumenschein Home**—On Ledoux Street one block south of the plaza, this 1797 adobe house was the home and studio of Ernest Blumenschein, a founder in 1915 of the Taos Society of Artists. Changing art exhibits, European antiques, and handmade Taos furniture are on display. Open daily from 9:00 a.m. to 5:00 p.m.; admission $2.50 for adults, $2 for senior citizens, $1.50 for children ages 6 to 15.

▲▲ **Martinez Hacienda**—This is the only remaining Spanish colonial hacienda in New Mexico open to the public on a regular basis. Built in 1804 as a fortresslike refuge from Comanche raids, it has thick adobe walls and no exterior windows. To find it, follow Ranchitos Road west from the plaza until you reach the Rio Grande. The 21-room hacienda is on the riverbank. Open daily from 9:00 a.m. to 5:00 p.m.; admission $2.50 for adults, $2 for senior citizens, $1.50 for children ages 6 to 15.

▲▲▲ **Taos Pueblo**—The oldest and best-known of the Rio Grande Indian pueblos, now a National Historic Landmark, preserves the multistory architectural style that dates back to the twelfth century. About 1,400 people live in the pueblo today. Ceremonies and dances held at the pueblo include the Fiesta of San Antonio on June 13, a corn dance in late June, a three-day powwow in early July, and the Fiesta of San Geronimo on the evening of September 29 and all day September 30. Call the pueblo at (505) 758-8626 for more information. To reach the pueblo, continue north from the plaza on NM 68 for about 2 miles and watch for the turnoff on your right. A $5 parking fee is charged, and photography fees are $5 for still cameras and $10 for movie or video cameras; no cameras are allowed during ceremonies.

▲ **Millicent Rogers Museum**—Founded in 1953 and relocated to its present building in 1968, this museum houses one of the most extensive private collections of Indian art in the Southwest. Featured are Navajo and Pueblo jewelry, Navajo textiles, Pueblo pottery and paintings, Hopi and Zuñi kachinas, and basketry from several Native American cultures as well as some Spanish colonial folk art items. To get there, go 4 miles north of Taos on the main highway; turn left just before the blinking light and follow the signs. Open daily from 9:00 a.m. to 5:00 p.m. May-October, 10:00 a.m. to 4:00 p.m. Wednesday through Sunday at other times of year; admission $3 for adults, $1 for children ages 6 to 16 and senior citizens.

▲ **D. H. Lawrence Ranch**—The British novelist, whose books stirred controversy on both sides of the Atlantic, took refuge here during 1924-25 to escape public notoriety. His widow, Frieda, willed the ranch to the University of New Mexico on condition that ten acres of the property, including the ranch buildings and shrine, always remain open to the public. While Lawrence never wrote a major work with a New Mexico setting, writers and readers from all over the world visit to draw inspiration from the Lawrence Shrine. Lawrence's ashes may be blended into the concrete slab in the shrine. (Somebody's are, anyway. So the story goes, there was a mix-up of urns at U.S. Customs in New York when the ashes were being brought from France. An appropriate postscript to an enigmatic life.) To reach the ranch, take the marked turnoff on the left, about 7 miles north of Taos on NM 68. The shrine is 100 yards uphill from the visitor parking area.

Besides writing, Lawrence once tried his hand at the visual arts. Amateurish though his attempts may have been, his paintings scandalized London and resulted in an obscenity prosecution that drove him from England for the last time. You can view the naughty pictures and judge for yourself for a dollar in a back room of La Fonda de Taos on the town plaza.

▲ **Rio Grande Gorge Bridge**—The only bridge across the gorge, affording a spectacular view of this stretch of the Rio Grande protected under the federal Wild and Scenic Rivers Act, is on US 64 (the highway to Tres Piedras), about 10 miles west of the intersection with NM 68, which is 4 miles north of Taos.

Travel Route: Taos to Great Sand Dunes National Monument (130 miles)

From Taos, continue north on NM 68 (which becomes CO 159 as it crosses the state line) for 79 miles, following the Sangre de Cristo Mountains along the eastern side of the San Luis Valley through San Luis, Colorado's oldest town, founded in 1851. The small museum and cultural center in San Luis contains an excellent exhibit, funded by the National Endowment for the Humanities, explaining the history of the valley and its people. CO 159 joins US 160 near Fort Garland, an 1850s U.S. Army outpost once commanded by Kit Carson and now a Colorado State Historic Site. This route is known as the Kit Carson Highway.

Though just up the river from Taos, the San Luis Valley wasn't explored by the Spanish for nearly two centuries. In 1779, the conquistador De Anza braved hostile Comanche bands to make it up as far as Alamosa, where the Rio Grande veers west to its headwaters in the San Juan Mountains. The discovery astonished mapmakers of the time, who had always assumed that the river came from the North Pole. U.S. Army occupation in the mid-1800s made the valley safe for Hispanic settlers, whose descendants live there today.

From Fort Garland, turn left (west) on US 160 and go 10 miles to the turnoff on the right (north) to Great Sand Dunes National Monument. From there, it's 16 miles to the monument entrance gate.

Great Sand Dunes National Monument

Like a beach in reverse, a wide shallow ribbon of cold mountain stream water lies along the edge of a vast and awesome expanse of sand. Beyond the picnic area turnoff near the visitors center, a mostly local crowd basks on beach towels beside beer coolers while the kids construct sand castles along the creek. It could be time to break out the bathing suits, even though the water is only two inches deep.

The sand dunes, the largest in the United States, formed as millennia of sandstorms swept the San Luis Valley, as they still do, dropping their loads of sand in a pile where the wind funnels into the mountains. The dunes are 900 feet high and cover an area of 60 square miles. To get a sense of how big the dunes really are, take out your binoculars and watch tiny hikers struggle toward the summits. For an even better sense, climb one yourself (allow two hours up, half an hour back) and, when you finally reach the top, you'll be rewarded by a view of many more miles of sand. A less crowded dune area is reached by a trail that leads from the campground past where escape dunes have engulfed the ponderosa forest.

Often used as an "alien planet" location for science fiction movies, the dunes also offer incomparable photographic opportunities. Particularly in early morning and late afternoon as shadows deepen, their weird abstractions challenge the eye. No two photographers' pictures of the sand dunes look alike. When hiking on the sand, wrap your camera in a plastic bag to protect the lens and mechanism from grit.

Entrance to the monument is $5 unless you have a Golden Eagle or Golden Age pass. Open year-round.

Camping

The 88-site **Piñon Flats Campground** at Great Sand
Dunes National Monument has tables, fire grills, convenient rest rooms, and nightly campfire talks. All campsites have fine views of the dunes. Deer are abundant and
may bound right through your camp. The campground
area also teems with chipmunks, ground squirrels, and
cottontail rabbits. Both the dunes trail and the Medano
Pass Primitive Road that intersects it are ideal for sunset
walking. The camping fee is $5. There are no hookups.

Full hookups are available at the **Great Sand Dunes
Oasis** outside the park for $11.50. They also offer horse-
back riding and four-wheel-drive tours into the backcountry dunes.

Within the park, backcountry camping is allowed (free
permit required, campfires prohibited) at **Sand Pit** and
Castle Creek, 1½ and 2 miles up Medano Creek Primitive Road. Unless you have four-wheel drive, don't even
think of driving on this road—the minimum tow charge
for getting unstuck from the sand is $100. If you're fully
equipped for backpacking, there is a hikers-only campground a quarter-mile from the road at mile 4.

Lodging

Alamosa, 32 miles from Great Sand Dunes, is your best
bet for motel accommodations. The **Best Western
Alamosa Inn**, 1919 Main Street, (719) 589-2567, has an
indoor pool; doubles start below $50. The **Holiday Inn**,
333 Santa Fe Avenue, (719) 589-5833, also has an indoor
pool as well as a sauna and whirlpool. Rates start at $56.
Lower-priced lodging can be found at the **Econo Lodge**,
425 Main Street, (303) 589-6636, where doubles start at
just over $30. All three motels have cable color television.

A gentleman from Washington, D.C., who used the first
edition of *22 Days in the American Southwest* enthusi-
astically recommends the new **Cottonwood Inn** at 123
San Juan Avenue in Alamosa. Although his suggestion
came too late for me to check it out, he calls it "one

of the nicest and best-run bed and breakfasts that we stayed in anywhere." For rates and reservations, call (719) 589-3882.

Food

I hope you brought some. Otherwise, a limited selection of groceries and microwave sandwiches is available at the **Great Sand Dunes Oasis** store. The nearest restaurant to Great Sand Dunes is the unpretentious little roadside café at Fort Garland.

DAY 5

OVER THE MOUNTAINS TO MESA VERDE

Since you left Albuquerque, you've followed the Rio Grande north for over 250 miles. Today you'll head west across the Great Divide to the Four Corners region, so called because the conjunction of Colorado, New Mexico, Arizona, and Utah—marked by a small monument (which isn't worth going out of your way for) beside US 160 an hour's drive southwest of Mesa Verde—is the only place in the United States where four states meet. Durango is the region's major town and tourism center. You'll spend most of today driving there.

Suggested Schedule

8:00 a.m.	Hike the dunes.
10:30 a.m.	Drive to Antonito.
12:30 p.m.	Drive to Chama, Cumbres Pass picnic.
2:30 p.m.	Drive to Durango.
5:00 p.m.	Drive to Mesa Verde and camp, or spend the night in Durango.

Travel Route: Sand Dunes to Mesa Verde—Direct (238 miles) or Scenic (304 miles)

Leaving Great Sand Dunes National Monument by the same 16-mile road you came in on, turn right (west) on US 160 and drive 16 more miles into Alamosa (pop. 7,000), the largest town in the San Luis Valley. There, at the junction of US 160 and US 285, you face a choice.

Durango lies on the other side of the Continental Divide, at the southwestern edge of the San Juan Mountains, the massive range you see to the west. The well-trodden tourist trail from Alamosa to Durango follows US 160 the whole way, about a 4-hour drive. The main scenic attraction on the route, and at the same time the major drawback, is 10,850-foot Wolf Creek Pass. Legendary among truck drivers, it's Colorado's highest and steepest mountain pass on a major highway. On the

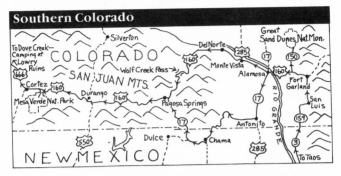

ascent, you may see (or join) numerous tourist vehicles overheated by the roadside. The long runaway truck ramp on the descent is there for a reason: be very careful not to "ride" your vehicle's brakes, which will overheat them and cause them to fail. This pass can pose a formidable obstacle to motor homes. Traffic may distract you from the scenery.

I suggest you try the much less traveled route over La Manga and Cumbres passes (10,230 feet and 10,022 feet). While these twin passes aren't much lower than Wolf Creek, the climb is more gradual. The relaxing drive through high mountain meadows is worth the extra 1½ hours of driving time. From Alamosa, turn left and follow US 285 straight south to Antonito (28 miles). Turn right (west) on State Highway 17 toward Chama. The highway climbs up from the San Luis Valley into San Juan National Forest, first following the Conejos River past a series of campgrounds and fishing spots, then ascending into the alpine meadows. At the top you'll see the tracks of the Cumbres & Toltec Scenic Railroad, which runs between Antonito and Chama by a different route. At the far end of the grassy slopes, just before you begin your descent, stand the train station, snowshed, and other abandoned buildings of Cumbres, a railroad ghost town from the 1880s. Descend into New Mexico. The road distance from Antonito to Chama is 48 miles.

At the junction about a mile south of Chama, just a few miles over the state line, turn right on US 84, which climbs back up into the national forest to Pagosa Springs, Colorado, 49 miles away. There, rejoin US 160 westbound to Durango (60 miles). Mesa Verde National Park is 36 miles past Durango on US 160.

Durango

Durango, a lively town of about 12,000 people, got its start in 1880 as a rail hub serving local ranches as well as gold and silver mines in the mountains to the north. Today, Durango thrives on tourism. The downtown historic district, centered around the D&SNG railroad station and the Strater Hotel, has been prettified far beyond its original Victorian splendor. Besides being close to Mesa Verde, Durango attracts year-round tourism with its famous narrow gauge railroad, Purgatory ski area (which has an alpine slide in the summertime), the annual Iron Horse Bicycle Race, rafting, fishing, cross-country skiing, and a host of other outdoor recreation possibilities.

In recent years, Durango has attracted an impressive number of fine artists and craftsmen, whose creations can be seen in at least 15 galleries and shops on and near Main Avenue between Fifth and Eleventh streets. The Durango Arts Center at 970 Main Avenue (259-2606) exhibits works by local artists and serves as a ticket outlet for the performing arts in the area.

Camping

Morefield Campground in Mesa Verde National Park is located 5 miles up the steep road from the park entrance. It's a huge campground—177 tent sites, 300 trailer/RV sites. Besides all the usual campground amenities, there are pay showers nearby at the grocery store. Camping costs $5 plus park admission. Campfire programs are presented nightly. The Knife Edge Trail, which starts at the edge of the campground, takes you out to a cliff view point ideal for sunset watching. Returning in the dusk, you're likely to see dozens of deer grazing in the meadow.

If the campground at Mesa Verde is full or you'd prefer to sleep with fewer fellow campers around, at **Lowry**

Ruins Historic Site you may find yourself all alone. Operated by the Bureau of Land Management, the site is not marked on most road maps and is known to only the most dedicated Indian ruins buffs. There is no admission or camping fee, no ranger on duty, and no water, so be sure you have plenty aboard. To get to Lowry Ruins, continue on US 160 10 miles beyond the Mesa Verde turnoff to the town of Cortez, and from there go north 19 miles on US 666 to Pleasant View, where a small road goes west (left) 9 miles to the ruins.

Lodging

Far View Motor Lodge is located in Mesa Verde National Park, midway along the park road near Far View Visitor Center. Rates are about $60, the views are magnificent, and there is a good restaurant at the lodge as well as a cafeteria at the visitors center. For current prices and reservations, contact ARA Mesa Verde Company, Box 277, Mancos, CO 81328, (303) 529-4421.

Durango has an abundance of hotels and motels in all price ranges. The finest is the **Strater Hotel**, the four-story brick centerpiece of downtown Durango's historic restoration district, at 699 Main Avenue. Dating back to 1887, the Strater has been undergoing room-by-room restoration for over 20 years. Guest rooms feature antique walnut furnishings, and public areas include a playhouse where melodramas are performed from June through September and an elegant Old West saloon. For reservations, call toll-free (800) 227-4431 in Colorado or (800) 247-4431 nationwide. Doubles start around $75 in the summer months, $55 off-season.

Moderately priced motels are concentrated along North Main Avenue (US 550 northbound). Good bets are the **Caboose Motel**, 3363 N. Main Avenue, (303) 247-1191, and the **Alpine Motel**, 3515 N. Main Avenue, (303) 247-4042. Both have doubles starting at about $32 with cable TV.

Food

Durango has even more restaurants per capita than Santa Fe but no distinctive regional cuisine. Cruise the streets of town and pick a place that suits your mood. It costs less than you might expect to dine in an antique-filled Victorian atmosphere at **Henry's**, the Strater Hotel's restaurant. Steak or seafood dinners range between $10 and $20. It will be more than a week before you find another restaurant in the Southwest as splurge-worthy as this one.

Itinerary Options

If you have an extra day to spend in southwestern Colorado, consider a day trip on either of two restored narrow gauge railroads.

The **Cumbres & Toltec Scenic Railroad** runs between Antonito, Colorado, and Chama, New Mexico, along a different route than the highway described in the Travel Route above. The train runs round-trips from either town to the midpoint at Osier ($27 adult, $10 for children 11 and under), and one-way train trips for the full length of the route with return transportation by van (adults $41.50, children $20). Make reservations well in advance through the Antonito depot, P.O. Box 668, Antonito, CO 81120, (719) 376-5483, or the Chama depot, P.O. Box 789, Chama, NM 87520, (505) 756-2151.

The San Juan Mountains north of Durango, the most spectacular in the Colorado Rockies, bear a striking resemblance to the Swiss Alps. I wish I could fit them into this 22-day itinerary, but they're just too big. The **Durango & Silverton Narrow Gauge Railroad** runs between Durango and the old mining/lumbering town of Silverton high in the mountains, round-trip only. Fares are $28.10 for adults, $14.10 for children 11 and under; there is also a Parlor Car, serving alcoholic beverages, with a higher fare of $48.30. The D&SNG is one of Colorado's most popular tourist attractions, and reservations should be made months in advance if possible.

Contact D&SNG, 479 Main Avenue, Durango, CO 81301, (303) 247-2733.

The **Million Dollar Highway** (US 550), north from Durango through Silverton to Ouray, rivals the train trip for scenery. The road distance is 72 miles each way. It doesn't sound like far, but plan on an all-day trip. The highway is paved but steep and curvy. If you're traveling in a large motor home, you will find riding the D&SNG train to Silverton more relaxing and economical than driving.

You'll find complete details on touring the San Juan Mountains and the Durango region in this book's companion volume, *22 Days in the Rockies* by Roger Rapoport.

DAY 6
MESA VERDE

Today, you'll begin exploring the ruins left behind by the remote ancestors of the ancient and modern Pueblo Indians you saw in the Santa Fe-Los Alamos-Taos area. The Anasazi people thrived in the Four Corners area for seven centuries until, 800 years ago, they suddenly vanished from the region. Today, their monumental cliff dwellings at Mesa Verde are a popular, often crowded national park.

Suggested Schedule

9:00 a.m.	Drive to the museum on Chapin Mesa. (If you're staying in Durango rather than in Mesa Verde National Park, start an hour earlier.)
10:00 a.m.	Visit the museum and learn about the people who lived in these amazing cliff dwellings.
11:00 a.m.	Walk the trail behind the museum into Spruce Tree Canyon.
1:00 p.m.	Did you bring picnic supplies? If not, grab a quick bite at the snack bar near the museum or drive back to Far View Visitor Center, where there is a cafeteria.
Afternoon	Rent a bicycle at the museum for a leisurely tour of the cliff dwellings on Chapin Mesa, then finish your day with a hike from the museum out to Petroglyph Point. Or, the less athletic may wish to tour Chapin Mesa by car and then return to Far View Visitor Center for a drive out to Wetherill Mesa.
Evening	Spend a second night in the park or in Durango.

The Anasazi

"Anasazi" is a Navajo word meaning "ancestors of our enemies" (the National Park Service translates it more politely as "ancient ones"). It is the name given to the ancestors of the Pueblo Indians who lived in the Four Corners area until the twelfth century A.D. Of several distinct Anasazi groups, the three largest were the Mesa Verde and Chaco cultures, whose cities you'll see today and tomorrow, and the Kayenta people who built the cliff dwellings at Navajo National Monument (Day 9).

The Anasazi lived at the northernmost reach of trade routes established by the Toltecs and other great civilizations of Mexico, so they learned agricultural, architectural, and other technologies much earlier than did tribes in other parts of northern America. Their religion, too, evolved from Mexican origins. From about A.D. 1000 on, the Anasazi had the largest cities north of the tropics on the American continent.

In the twelfth century, within one or two generations, the Anasazi abandoned their pueblos one after another until the Four Corners area was virtually unpopulated. Nobody knows why. War? Disease? Drought? Wanderlust? Anthropologists argue endlessly. The current theory is that overpopulation brought soil depletion, erosion, and environmental disaster. The mysterious fall of the Anasazi empire is worthy of meditation among the ruins.

Mesa Verde National Park

In 1906, when Mesa Verde was made a national park to protect the largest and most extensive cliff dwellings in North America, the rare horseback visitor must have found the experience of a lifetime. Today its immense popularity, necessitating crowd control to protect archaeological sites, channels many tourists into a few public areas, making Mesa Verde a congested place. Yet the magic of this piñon-covered island 2,000 feet in the sky, with its ancient, castlelike "lost cities," makes itself felt even in a crowd.

Start touring Mesa Verde early in the morning to beat the charter buses. Admission to the park is $5 per vehicle. After a long, steep climb to the mesa top (travel trailers must be left below at the entrance station parking area or at the campground) and a pause at Park Point, with its superb view of the Mancos and Montezuma valleys and the San Juan Mountains, midway along the park road you'll come to Far View Visitor Center, where you can find out the current schedule for ranger-guided walks. One of these walks, offered free by the National Park Service, can enhance your Mesa Verde experience with insights about the people who once lived here and the plants and animals that still do.

Sightseeing Highlights

▲▲ **Mesa Verde Museum**—This old stone museum at park headquarters on Chapin Mesa, 20 miles from the park entrance, contains dioramas that show how civilization evolved on Mesa Verde during the same time period as Europe's Dark Ages. Take time to admire the museum's collection of ancient pottery, with its fine craftsmanship and elaborate geometric designs, and appreciate the thousand-year artistic heritage behind the Pueblo pottery you saw (and may have bought) in Albuquerque, Santa Fe, and Taos. The museum is open daily from 8:00 a.m. to 5:00 p.m., free.

▲▲▲ **Chapin Mesa Ruins**—Two separate loop roads begin at the museum on Chapin Mesa. Each road is about 3 miles round-trip and worth taking your time. Rent a bicycle at the museum, and the tour will seem even more spectacular. The major cliff dwellings are on the west loop, a left turn not far past the museum parking area. Of the many sites, **Cliff Palace** is the largest. It is accessible on a half-mile trail with a 500-foot climb; allow an hour. The walk to **Balcony House**, on the same road as it loops around to the other side of the mesa, means climbing a 32-foot ladder, ducking through a 12-foot tunnel, and ascending 100 feet up the cliff face. During crowded times, you can only see these two ruins on ranger-guided tours, which run frequently. The tour is well worth the wait.

▲▲ **Walking Trails**—If you want to escape the crowds at Mesa Verde, walk. Two trails begin at the museum, where you must obtain a free hiking permit. The permit system and many visitors' aversion to physical exercise keep the trails uncrowded—only one out of a thousand visitors hikes either trail. **Spruce Canyon Trail** is 2.1 miles long with a 700-foot climb down and back. **Petroglyph Point Trail** is 2.3 miles long with no steep climbing. Either takes about two hours round-trip.

▲ **Wetherill Mesa**—A 20-mile drive from the Far View Visitor Center leads to recently excavated mesa-top pueblo ruins. The area could only be reached by shuttle bus until recently but is now open to automobiles, a move the park service hopes will alleviate traffic congestion in the main ruins area on Chapin Mesa. Keep your eyes peeled for wild horses along the way.

AZTEC AND CHACO CANYON

Today's journey takes you to Anasazi ruins larger, more remote, and even more mysterious than those at Mesa Verde. If you are equipped to camp and have at least a day's worth of food aboard, you can take time to explore Chaco Canyon, the Southwest's premier Indian ruin, and let your imagination run free. (Otherwise, you'll have to speed up today's sightseeing in order to reach Interstate 40, where the nearest motels are, by nightfall.)

Suggested Schedule

9:30 a.m.	Drive south from Durango to Aztec. (Start an hour earlier if you spent last night at Mesa Verde National Park.)
10:00 a.m.	See Aztec National Monument.
11:30 a.m.	Drive to Angel Peak Recreation Area.
12:00 noon	Picnic.
1:00 p.m.	Drive to Chaco Canyon.
3:00 p.m.	Explore Chaco Canyon.
Evening	Camp at Chaco Canyon.

Travel Route: Mesa Verde to Aztec (71 miles)

From Mesa Verde National Park, return to Durango on US 160. Five miles east of Durango, where the highway forks, take US 550 south to Aztec. The total driving time from Mesa Verde to Aztec is 1½ hours.

The town of Aztec, population 6,000, won the National Municipal League's "All-American City" title in 1963 for building a 14-mile road to Navajo Lake—without help from any level of government. All funds, labor, and machinery were donated by local citizens. Aztec still takes the title to heart. A walk along the main street, with its small turn-of-the-century historic district and quaint local museum, can make you feel as if you'd slipped through time into Middle America, circa 1963.

Aztec Ruins National Monument is near the river, just

Anasazi Country

over the bridge from downtown Aztec on the road to Farmington, plainly marked with signs.

Aztec Ruins National Monument

Aztec Ruins, on the bank of the Animas River, was a large twelfth-century pueblo. Its name derives from early settlers' mistaken belief that this and other southwestern ruins were colonies from a higher civilization in Mexico. While the Anasazi traded with Mexican Toltecs and perhaps Aztecs for parrots and other items, and some construction techniques apparently originated in Mexico, Aztec was actually built by colonists from Chaco, 60 miles to the south. Abandoned during the decline of the Chaco culture, the pueblo was later reoccupied by people from Mesa Verde. Artifacts and architectural features from both Anasazi cultures invite side-by-side comparison. The showpiece of this national monument is the fully reconstructed great kiva, which will help you appreciate other kiva ruins, such as Chaco's Casa Rinconada, as prehistoric cathedrals, not just big holes in the ground. The short (400-yard) path through the ruins is open from 8:00 a.m. to 5:00 p.m. daily all year and to 6:30 p.m. June through August.

If these ruins fascinate you, consider a one-hour side trip to **Salmon Ruins**, a similar Chacoan outlier pueblo dating from the eleventh century, 12 miles from Aztec on the road between Farmington and Bloomfield. Open 9:00 a.m. to 5:00 p.m. daily all year.

Travel Route: Aztec to Chaco Canyon (61 miles)
Fill up with gas and check your food supply before leaving Aztec; you won't see another town until tomorrow. Drive south on NM 44 through the neighboring community of Bloomfield and out into the empty San Juan Basin.

Eighteen miles south of Aztec (13 miles past Bloomfield) on the left (east) is an unpaved road turnoff to **Angel Peak Recreation Area**. Angel Peak itself is easy to spot. It's the butte several miles to the east, crowned by a rock formation that, with imagination, resembles an angel with outspread wings. The sign marking the road that takes you there is less obvious. Drive in just half a mile to the first overlook and you'll be rewarded with a totally unexpected view of Kutz Canyon, a bright bit of red and white painted desert. There is a canyon rim picnic area 2 ½ miles farther down the road. A scenic free campground 2 miles beyond that has 16 rarely used camp-sites with rest rooms, picnic tables and grills, but no water.

Fifteen miles past the Angel Peak turnoff on NM 44 is Blanco Trading Post, where a clearly marked road turns off to the right (southwest) toward Chaco Culture National Historic Park. The road, unpaved and 30 miles long, will take an hour to drive under good road conditions. "Don't pave the road to Chaco Canyon" was an environmentalist rallying cry in the mid-1970s. The issue of paving the road is coming around again in the 1990s as Chaco Canyon becomes better known and more visited. Still, while hordes of tourists overrun Mesa Verde, Chaco's park rangers can usually relax with a few dozen adventuresome visitors. The road is normally an easy drive, thrilling for a minute as it plunges headlong into the canyon to let you know you're almost there. If there have been recent thunderstorms in the area, call Chaco headquarters, (505) 786-5384, for a road condition report before proceeding. When wet, parts of the clay road can be as slick as a skating pond.

The surrounding land is sparsely inhabited by Navajo people. While not officially part of the reservation, most ranches in the area have been purchased by the tribe and are regarded as part of the Navajo Nation. There is no gasoline, food, lodging, or repair service at Chaco, and the nearest town is the one you just came from, 60 miles away.

Chaco Culture National Historic Park

Until 1983, this site was called Chaco Canyon National Monument. Its new tongue twister name notwithstanding, most folks still just call it Chaco Canyon.

At Mesa Verde and Aztec, we can wonder why the Anasazi suddenly abandoned such beautiful spots. Chaco presents different archaeological mysteries. With so much wide open space around, why did the Chacoans cluster together into a mega-pueblo, the largest city the Anasazi ever saw, the Los Angeles of the prehistoric

Southwest? And why, of all places, here?

Even with its sophisticated irrigation system, Chacoans could not grow enough food to support the population of 5,000 but had to import it from outlier colonies. For vigas, or roof and floor supports in the pueblos, the people had to carry countless thousands of ponderosa logs from the mountains fifty miles away, a formidable task considering that they had no horses, nor had they knowledge of the wheel. Chacoans' abundant turquoise supply came from even farther away, in the Cerrillos hills near Santa Fe. While they made elaborate and distinctive black-on-white decorative pottery, most everyday cooking pots were imported. What did they give in exchange for all the imports needed to keep this city alive?

Archaeologists don't know. A clue may lie in the extraordinary number of kivas at Chaco, which suggest that it was a religious center. Natural beauty, the spirit of place, was probably important in the religion of the Anasazi, as it is to their Pueblo descendants today. Especially at twilight, one can readily imagine Chaco Canyon as sacred land.

The largest pueblo, Pueblo Bonito, rose four stories and contained 800 rooms. Besides all the excavated pueblos you see here, there are a number of others in the area that are crumbled and buried, recognizable only by differing vegetation. The Chaco people also established about 60 satellite pueblos called "outliers" throughout the San Juan Basin, from Aztec in the north to the Grants area in the south. The major outliers were connected by an 800-mile network of improved roads thirty feet wide, with Chaco at the hub.

Late afternoon or early morning is the best time to tour and photograph the ruins. For solitude and a different perspective on Chaco Canyon, hike the trail up to Tsin Kletsin ruins (4-mile, 2½-hour round-trip) on the canyon rim. The trail starts at Casa Rinconada, Chaco's largest great kiva.

Chaco Canyon is open year-round (road conditions permitting). No admission is charged.

Camping

Chaco's **Gallo Campground** is small, with only about two dozen established sites. A sign on the road into the park warns that the campground may fill up by 3:00 p.m. on weekends. The campground has tables, fireplaces, and rest rooms. The only water supply is at the visitors center, about half a mile away. Rangers present campfire programs nightly during the summer season.

Lodging

The closest motels to Chaco Canyon are in the Farmington-Bloomfield-Aztec area and the Grants-Gallup area, each two hours away. The only campground is the one in the park. Bring your own food.

Itinerary Option

If you have extra time and a yearning for water, head for **Navajo Lake**, New Mexico's largest lake, near Aztec. Pine River Marina, 23 miles east of Aztec on NM 511 not far above the dam, has the nearest campground and boat rental. More remote facilities are at Sims Mesa across the lake: turn left at the first fork in the road after you cross the dam. Empty except on weekends, Navajo Lake is a good place to rent a motorboat for a day or overnight back-canyon boat-camping trip. A 40-horsepower outboard rents for $10 an hour or $40 for 24 hours. A Kayot, a motorized raft with a roof which can carry four to six people, costs $20 an hour or $80 for 24 hours.

CHACO CANYON TO CANYON DE CHELLY

Leaving Chaco Canyon by a different unpaved road, you'll return to I-40 just two hours' drive from Albuquerque, where you started nearly a week ago. Then begin your tour of the largest Indian reservation in the United States with a visit to the tribal zoo and historic Hubbell Trading Post. You'll end the day at Canyon de Chelly, the heart of the land of the Navajo.

Suggested Schedule

9:00 a.m.	Leave Chaco Canyon.
11:00 a.m.	Take a break in Gallup. Fill the gas tank, stock up on food.
11:30 a.m.	Visit Navajo Tribal Zoological Park.
12:30 p.m.	Picnic at Window Rock Tribal Park.
1:15 p.m.	Drive to Ganado.
2:00 p.m.	See Hubbell Trading Post.
3:15 p.m.	Drive to Canyon de Chelly National Monument.
4:00 p.m.	Arrive at Canyon de Chelly, find a campsite or check into the lodge, and visit the visitors center.
5:00 p.m.	Take a late afternoon drive along the north rim of Canyon del Muerto.

Travel Route: Chaco Canyon to Canyon de Chelly (156 miles)

The road south out of Chaco Canyon doesn't take as long to reach the pavement—just 10 dusty miles. Continue south and west on NM 57 as it joins the Vietnam Veterans Memorial Highway near Crownpoint and, 32 miles later, reaches I-40 at the tiny town of Thoreau, midway between Grants and Gallup.

Take the interstate west for 33 miles to Gallup (pop. 20,000), the "border town" of the Navajo Nation. Existing primarily as a truck stop and railroad way station, Gallup has an old downtown area on the south side of the interstate and train tracks and a strip of shopping malls, supermarkets, and fast-food places on the north side. On the old side, pawn shops, curio shops, and trading companies sell Navajo and Zuñi arts and crafts at prices far lower than those in Albuquerque or Santa Fe. Some of the turn-of-the-century storefronts along Main Street have had recent face lifts to become galleries, but Gallup is a long way from becoming a touristy historic district. Restaurants and motels are, on the whole, budget-basic. Drunken Indians are a common sight at any time of day or night. Draw no general conclusions about Native Americans from encounters with these few; it's just that Gallup is the only place in the region where a man can get a drink if he craves one. Alcoholic beverages are illegal on the Navajo Reservation and hard to get beyond the reservation's northern boundary, in Utah, where anything stronger than beer is only sold in state liquor stores whose locations often seem like closely guarded secrets.

Take four-lane US 666 north from Gallup for 7 miles and turn west on Highway 264 to Window Rock, the Navajo Nation's capital (pop. 2,200). You will cross the Arizona state line shortly before entering town. Although the rest of Arizona stays on Mountain Standard Time while New Mexico, Colorado, and Utah observe daylight saving time, the entire Navajo Nation also goes on daylight saving time, so there is no need to reset your watch on this leg of the trip. (In fact, for the next few days there will be very little reason to consult your watch at all.)

From Window Rock, continue on Highway 264 for 34 more miles to reach Hubbell Trading Post, a mile past Ganado near the intersection with US 191. After visiting the trading post, turn north on US 191 and drive 31 miles to the turnoff for Chinle and Canyon de Chelly National Monument.

The Navajo Nation

The Navajo Nation encompasses nearly 16 million acres, an area larger than Connecticut, Massachusetts, and New

Hampshire combined. The eastern part of the reservation is mountainous evergreen forest with several recreation lakes; the center is the arid, piñon-covered Lukachukai Plateau; and the western part is painted desert. All land on the reservation is inhabited, a fact that is not obvious because the Navajo traditionally locate each house out of sight of any other house.

Athabascan Indians migrated from northwestern Canada to New Mexico and Arizona shortly before the Spanish did. Those who adopted new ways from the Pueblo people and Spanish settlers, such as sheepherding, weaving, and growing corn, came to be called Navajo (from a Pueblo word meaning "green planted fields"). The other Athabascans, who held to their older nomadic traditions, were called Apache.

In 1864, soon after the Navajo lands became U.S. territory (most reservation Navajo, young and old alike, talk as though it happened yesterday), Kit Carson's army burned the Navajo cornfields to starve the people out of hiding. Carson then marched the Navajo people, who then numbered about 8,000, along with 2,000 horses and 10,000 sheep and goats, for 300 miles to a camp at Fort Sumner in eastern New Mexico. Without supplies, many Navajo died along the trail. Famine plagued the Fort Sumner camps; meanwhile, American surveyors could find nothing desirable about the former Navajo lands. Four years later, the army marched the remaining Navajo and their flocks back home. The degrading experience fostered tribal unity, increased distrust of the white man, heightened belief in the special quality of their homeland, and galvanized the "Navajo Nation."

In a few scattered towns, twentieth-century conveniences such as pickup trucks, video rental stores, and government housing projects adorned by satellite TV antennas—new additions to the tribe's unique way of life—have all been borrowed from the American mainstream. Horses, sheep, corn, jewelry making, and weaving were all similarly borrowed to create the traditional Navajo life-style, and the process continues.

The more you travel in Navajoland, the more it may seem like a Third World country (though one with exceptional respect for the natural environment). Most Navajo people live away from towns and highways and have no electricity or running water. The tribe faces problems of poverty and overpopulation. The Navajo Nation, the largest tribe in the United States, now numbers about 200,000. Only 20 percent can live off the land, and of the rest, 85 percent are unemployed. Coal mines and natural gas wells provide tribal income and a few jobs but scar the land. Experimental reservation industries range from a pilot microchip plant (now closed) to cultivation of rare oriental mushrooms.

You'll see signs on the reservation for three kinds of places important in Navajo society—trading posts, chapterhouses, and missions.

Trading posts are general stores operated by traders

under federal license. They sell a selection of food some-
what more limited than 7-Eleven stores, as well as dry
goods, gasoline, and sometimes hay or feed for livestock.
Traditionally, traders also served as pawnbrokers, ex-
changing their wares for rugs and jewelry that they sold
to collectors, and some trading posts continue the practice. If you stop at enough trading posts, you'll find a fair
selection of Navajo handicrafts. For many Navajo it's a
long trip to the trading post, and once there, they like to
stay around for a good part of the day, talking with who-
ever else stops by.

Chapterhouses are the basic unit of Navajo tribal government. They serve the purpose of town meeting halls,
even though many are far from any town. Chapters elect
88 councilmen to represent them in the tribal council.
The Council Chambers, near Window Rock Tribal Park,
are open from 8:00 a.m. to 5:00 p.m. on many weekdays.
Visitors fortunate enough to find the council in session
will hear tribal issues debated in both English and Navajo.

Missions have been established throughout the reservation by a number of Christian denominations. The
first, at Ganado, was built by the Presbyterians under a
decree from President Grant which arbitrarily assigned
Indian reservations to various missionary groups. Since
the beginning of the twentieth century, other missionaries have included the Franciscan Order and the Meth-
odist and Christian Reformed churches. Visitors are welcome at all of them. Christian fundamentalist tent revivals,
too, are held frequently around the reservation. Some
feature Navajo preachers. If you come across one (audible
for miles, they're hard to miss), by all means join the
flock. Old-time evangelism among the Indians makes for
a unique and thought-provoking cultural experience
regardless of your personal faith. Traditional Navajo religious beliefs survive, and "sings"—healing ceremonies
that involve chanting and sand painting—still take place,
though non-Navajo visitors are rarely included.

Sightseeing Highlights

▲▲ Navajo Tribal Zoological Park—This low-budget zoo looks like a combination barnyard and humane society shelter, but don't let first impressions put you off. Here you'll feel the Navajo people's unique attitude toward animals. Sheep and other domestic animals roam throughout the grounds, while wild animals (most were found injured and brought here from other parts of the reservation) are kept in wire pens to protect them from tourists. Signs name each animal in both English and Navajo, and a display in the visitors center tells a little bit about the animals' mythological roles as spiritual forefathers of the various Navajo clans. Among the zoo's residents are a black bear, a mountain lion, a wolf, birds of prey, and sometimes bison. Located off Arizona 264, a half-mile east of Window Rock Shopping Center, the zoo is open daily from 8:00 a.m. to 5:00 p.m.; 50 cents per person donation requested.

▲ Navajo Tribal Museum—Exhibits depict Navajo history. There are also Anasazi artifacts and a large arts and crafts shop. On Arizona 264 between the shopping center and Window Rock Motor Inn, the museum is open Monday through Friday, 8:00 a.m. to 4:45 p.m., free.

▲ Window Rock Tribal Park—The rock formation for which the Navajo capital was named is ½ mile east (right) off Tribal Route 12, ½ mile north of Arizona 264. There are picnic tables, rest rooms, water, and a walking trail.

▲▲ Hubbell Trading Post National Historic Site—John Lorenzo Hubbell, the New Mexico-born son of a U.S. soldier, founded this trading post in 1878. It became the center of his Navajo Reservation trade empire, which grew to include 24 trading posts as well as stage and freight lines. Arriving among the Navajo soon after the second Long Walk, as the people were struggling to adjust to reservation life, Hubbell served as the Indians' spokesman and contact with the white world for over 50 years. He wrote, "The first duty of an Indian trader is to advise them to produce that which their natural inclina-

tions and talent best adapts them, to find a market for
their products and vigilantly watch that they keep im-
proving in the production of same, and advise them
which commands the best price." Hubbell encouraged
the Navajo to develop the high-quality rug weaving and
silversmithing for which they are known today.

Hubbell Trading Post, the oldest continuously active
trading post on the reservation, still sells food and dry
goods to the Indians and excellent-quality Navajo goods
to tourists. Weavers and silversmiths demonstrate their
arts at the visitors center. Take a free guided tour of Hubbell's home and grounds. Both the trading post and the
visitors center are open daily from 8:00 a.m. to 6:00 p.m.
in the summer, 8:00 a.m. to 5:00 p.m. the rest of the year.

▲▲▲ **Canyon de Chelly National Monument: North
Rim (Canyon del Muerto)**—Taking the north rim drive
this evening and seeing the south rim—which is a different canyon—tomorrow morning will let you make the
most of the fairly limited automobile sightseeing possibilities at Canyon de Chelly National Monument. The overlooks along the two scenic drives afford the only views
you get of Canyon de Chelly and Canyon del Muerto
unless you take a horseback trip into the canyon with a
Navajo guide (see "Itinerary Options"). Traditional Navajo herdsmen live in hogans below the sheer, impassable
cliffs, seemingly oblivious to the tourists who daily peer
down at them from the rim. To explore the canyon, use
binoculars.

Canyon de Chelly (the name, pronounced "d'SHAY," is
an Anglo mispronunciation of a Spanish misspelling of
Tsegi, Navajo for "rock canyon") is the traditional center
of the Navajo lands. According to their mythology, the
Navajo people and animals emerged into the world from
this place.

Canyon de Chelly National Monument headquarters
area has a visitors center (open daily, 8:00 a.m. to 7:00
p.m. May through September, 8:00 a.m. to 5:00 p.m.
October to April), campground, and lodge. There is no

admission fee to Canyon de Chelly. Various brochures available at the visitors center cost fifty cents each. Tribal Road 64 goes from the park headquarters area to the small Navajo college town of Tsaile, 35 miles away, but sightseers need only drive the first 18 miles to see all the view points along the north rim of Canyon del Muerto, then return by the same route. Five miles up the road from the visitors center is **Ledge Ruin Viewpoint**, an unexcavated Anasazi ruin that had about fifty rooms and two kivas. Three miles farther up the road is **Antelope House Overlook**, named for the paintings of antelope on the canyon wall to the left of the ruin, probably painted by a Navajo artist in the early nineteenth century. Nearby paintings of hands and other figures are from the Anasazi people who lived here as early as the seventh century.

Ten more miles up the road will bring you to a turnoff on your right (south) to **Mummy Cave** and **Massacre Cave** overlooks. Mummy Cave is the site of one of the largest Anasazi ruins in the canyon, a 77-room, Mesa Verde-style cliff dwelling with a three-story tower. Discovery in the 1880s of two mummies buried at this site gave the canyon its name (which means "Canyon of the Dead"). Massacre Cave was so named because a Spanish expedition slaughtered 115 Indians here in 1805.

Camping
Canyon de Chelly's **Cottonwood Campground**, half a mile from the visitors center, has rest rooms, picnic tables, water, and a dumping station but no hookups or showers. Camping is free. Rangers present campfire programs nightly during the summer months.

Lodging
Rooms at Canyon de Chelly's **Thunderbird Lodge**, near the visitors center and campground, range from $57 to $64 double. **Canyon de Chelly Motel**, 1½ miles away on the outskirts of Chinle, has rooms for $68.

Food

The cafeteria at **Thunderbird Lodge**, open 7:00 a.m. to
8:30 p.m., serves good food at moderate prices. Try a
Navajo taco—Indian-style fry bread heaped with meat,
beans, lettuce, and cheese. Although $4.50 might sound
like a high price for a taco, this one will fill you up with
some left over. Navajo sand paintings displayed in the cafeteria are among the finest you'll see anywhere.

Nearby, Chinle has a shopping center with a supermarket as well as two local cafés and a **Kentucky Fried
Chicken**.

Helpful Hints

Tourist brochures warn that traditional Navajo may refuse
to talk to non-Indian tourists, but my experience has
been that most people on the reservation are quite will-
ing to talk with outsiders. What may seem like shyness or
unfriendliness is actually cultural difference: Navajo people are taught from childhood not to talk too much, be
loud, or start conversations with strangers, and eye contact while speaking is considered impolite. A good way to
meet an Indian who doesn't work in the tourist trade is to
offer a ride to a hitchhiker. It's safe (but use discretion on
the highway from Gallup to Window Rock). Hitching
rides is common on the reservation, because there is no
public transportation.

While a few older people on the reservation speak no
English, nearly all Navajo, young and old alike, are bilin-
gual. Despite early attempts by the U.S. government to
eradicate it through boarding school education, the
Navajo language is now a source of patriotic and tribal
pride thanks largely to the "Code-talkers," 1,500 Navajo
men who broadcast secret military messages among
Pacific islands during World War II. Navajo was the only
American "code" the Japanese never succeeded in
deciphering. Listen to spoken Navajo as you drive across
the reservation. Several area radio stations have Navajo-
language programming at different times throughout the

day. Try KTNN Window Rock, 660 on your AM radio dial.

Free camping or driving on back roads is a bad idea on the Navajo Reservation. Any time you leave the pavement, you're trespassing on somebody's grazing land, and back roads are usually somebody's driveway. Back roads on the reservation are often in terrible condition, easy to get stuck or lost on. Never enter a hogan or other home uninvited. If you need help, observe Navajo tradition and stop at least 50 yards away, call, then wait until someone comes out to see what you want. Respect for privacy helps ensure that the tribe will continue to welcome visitors.

Two major Native American events take place in the Gallup/Window Rock area in the late summer, and either is worth planning your trip around. The Inter-Tribal Ceremonial and Rodeo, the largest Indian powwow in the nation, takes place Thursday through Sunday the second weekend in August at Red Rocks State Park near Gallup; call (505) 863-3896 for complete information. The Navajo Nation Fair, the Navajo equivalent of a state fair with contest dancing, a rodeo, concerts, carnival rides, and a large, fascinating arts and crafts pavilion, is held Thursday through Sunday of the week following Labor Day. Since it is held on the same weekend as Santa Fe's much better known Fiesta, hardly any non-Indian tourists are among the 80,000 people who visit the Navajo Nation Fair each year.

Itinerary Options

Visitors are only allowed down into Canyon de Chelly or Canyon del Muerto when accompanied by Navajo guides, to protect the ancient ruins, the present-day residents' privacy, and you (from quicksand and flash floods), but you can arrange guided tours. The most exciting option is a one-day horseback trip up-canyon to Mummy Cave or Antelope House, $40 per person. Call **Twin Trail Tours** at (602) 871-4663 for information and reservations, or inquire at the visitors center. Four-wheel-drive tours can be arranged at **Thunderbird Lodge**, $23 ($17 for children under 12) for a half-day or $39 all day. Navajo guides to accompany you up-canyon on a hike or in your own four-wheel-drive vehicle can be arranged through **Tsegi Guide Association** at the visitors center, $6 per hour.

CANYON DE CHELLY TO
MONUMENT VALLEY

For a close-up look at traditional Navajo life, drive from Canyon de Chelly in the heart of the Navajo Nation toward the reservation's northern boundary on the edge of Utah's uninhabited slickrock country and visit Monument Valley Tribal Park.

Suggested Schedule

8:00 a.m.	Breakfast.
9:00 a.m.	Canyon de Chelly south rim drive.
10:30 a.m.	Drive to Kayenta.
11:30 a.m.	Drive to Navajo National Monument. Picnic and see Betatakin ruins.
2:00 p.m.	Drive to Monument Valley.
3:30 p.m.	Explore Monument Valley.
5:00 p.m.	Camp at Monument Valley or stay at Goulding's Trading Post.

Travel Route: Chinle to Monument Valley (104 miles)

Leaving Canyon de Chelly, take US 191 north from Chinle for 15 miles to the barely noticeable community of Many Farms, and turn left (west) there on Tribal Route 59. A 58-mile drive along the base of Black Mesa will bring you to US 160. Turn left (west again) and go 8 miles to Kayenta. To visit Navajo National Monument, continue west on US 160 for 22 miles, then go 9 miles north on Arizona 564. After visiting Navajo National Monument, retrace your route back to Kayenta. From Kayenta to Monument Valley is 23 miles via US 163.

Sightseeing Highlights

▲▲▲ **Canyon de Chelly National Monument: South Rim**—Take the 22-mile (each way) scenic drive from the visitors center along the south rim of the canyon. Tsegi

Overlook, 2.5 miles along the road, affords an excellent
view of traditional hogans and farms on the canyon floor,
and 1.4 miles beyond that is Junction Overlook, where
you can see two early Anasazi ruins. Two miles farther on
is White House Overlook; about 150 yards to the right of
the overlook is the only nonguided hiking trail into Canyon de Chelly, a two-hour, 2 ½ -mile round-trip, 500-foot
descent to the large White House Ruin. Bring water. Fifteen miles from there, at the upper end of the canyon, is
the overlook for Spider Rock, a solitary 800-foot pinnacle on top of which, according to legend, Spider Woman
lives. Not a comic book character, Spider Woman is the
mythological being who taught Navajo women the art of
weaving. Spider Rock is the last stop on the south rim
scenic drive. Return to the visitors center the same way
you came.

▲ **Navajo National Monument**—The monument protects major cliff dwellings of the Kayenta culture, the
third major Anasazi group (the others being the Chaco
and Mesa Verde cultures). The only easily accessible ruin
is Betatakin, which can be seen from the easy one-mile
trail that starts at the visitors center. If you have extra
time, consider a guided 16-mile wilderness hike or horseback trip into the backcountry to see Keet Seel, the
largest cliff dwelling in Arizona and one of the best
preserved anywhere. Keet Seel was occupied for only 25
years, yet centuries later, charcoal remains in the hearths,
and there are dried ears of corn in the grain storage
rooms. For information and reservations, contact Navajo
National Monument, H.C. 63, Box 3, Tonalea, AZ 86044,
(602) 672-2366. Horseback trips cost about $40 per per-
son. The number of visitors to Keet Seel is limited to 25
per day, so make reservations well in advance.

▲▲▲ **Monument Valley Navajo Tribal Park**—A combination of strange landscape, traditional Navajo life, and
sincere if humble tribal hospitality gives the valley a special quality that is unrivaled. As you overlook Monument
Valley from the visitors center, you may be struck by déjà

vu. This desert landscape, with its spirelike buttes and mesas, has been background scenery for so many Western movies, TV shows, and commercials that you'll recognize it instantly. John Ford's Point is named after the director of *Stagecoach* (1938), the first motion picture ever filmed here.

Taking the 17-mile unpaved road through the valley seems like driving through a movie, too. Along the way you'll discover the real magic of Monument Valley: people live here. This is not an open-air folk museum, and the people have not been hired to look picturesque for tourists. Their families happened to live here when Monument Valley became a tribal park in 1958, and they still do. Of approximately 100 Navajo who make their homes in Monument Valley, most are descendants of families who fled here a century ago to escape the Long March.

Today, Monument Valley residents thrive on tourism. Even with nearly a million visitors a year, the quiet curio business makes a delightful counterpoint to high-pressure hype encountered in places such as Las Vegas. Many things still cost only a dollar, though worth far more. Beside one roadside ramada where a twelve-year-old Navajo girl offers cedar-bead necklaces, a sign handwritten on cardboard reads: "Beads and rug for sale. Taken picture of the girls or woman weaving you pay them $1.00 each for each of them. look inside hogan is $1.00 per person and taken pix of hogans $1.00 too. Thanx."

A guided tour is worthwhile in Monument Valley, since some roads are for four-wheel-drive tour vehicles only. Of several tours available at the visitors center, I recommend **Navajo Guided Tour Service**, the only company whose owner-operators were born and raised in Monument Valley. All of their tours cover the same 28-mile backcountry route, including Anasazi ruins, petroglyphs, and a visit to the guide's grandmother's hogan. Longer trips proceed at a slower pace. Two-hour trips run $15/person; half-day, $20/person; full-day, $30/person including lunch. Plus $1 per person ($0.50 for kids) for the grandmother. Sunrise and sunset trips cost slightly more. For more information, contact Frank or Linda Rodriguez, 450 East Pinion Road, #7, Blanding, UT 84511, (801) 678-2360. Monument Valley's visitors center and scenic drive are open from 7:00 a.m. to 7:00 p.m. May through September, 8:00 a.m. to 5:00 p.m. October to April. Admission is $1 per person.

Camping
Monument Valley has a 100-site campground that, according to officials there, is never full. The camping fee is $7 plus park admission. The campsites are small and close together, but there is boundless open space for evening desert walking nearby. Best of all, the central rest rooms have pay showers.

Lodging
Goulding's Lodge and Trading Post, (801) 727-3231, is in the opposite direction from the Monument Valley entrance gate, two miles west of US 163. The historic trading post has been operated by the same family for almost seventy years. Rooms run about $78 a night during tourist season. Goulding's also has a grocery store, a service station, and good-quality Navajo handicrafts.

TRAIL OF THE ANCIENTS TO CANYONLANDS

Escalante National Park was proposed by conservationists in the 1930s. The plan was rejected. If it had passed, it would have protected over 7,000 square miles of southern Utah in one of the nation's largest parks. Though some of the land has been lost under the water of Lake Powell, many sightseeing highlights of would-be Escalante National Park are now state parks, national monuments, or national parks in their own right. Tour them today and tomorrow. Take the Trail of the Ancients north to Moab, Utah. Camp tonight on the Island in the Sky in the center of Canyonlands National Park, and explore Arches National Park this afternoon or tomorrow morning.

Suggested Schedule

8:00 a.m.	Drive to Natural Bridges National Monument.
9:30 a.m.	Natural Bridges scenic drive and hike.
11:30 a.m.	Drive to Blanding.
12:30 p.m.	Picnic at Devil's Canyon.
1:30 p.m.	Drive to Monticello.
2:00 p.m.	Drive to Moab.
4:00 p.m.	Drive to Canyonlands.
5:00 p.m.	Explore Island in the Sky. Camp at Canyonlands or Dead Horse Point, or spend the night in Moab.

Travel Route: Monument Valley to Natural Bridges (64 miles)

From Monument Valley, go northeast on US 163 for 26 miles, passing through the small town of Mexican Hat, Utah, on the Navajo Reservation boundary line. Just north of town on your right you'll see the town's namesake—a rock formation that looks like an upside-down sombrero.

Soon after you pass the hat, turn left (west) on UT 261, known as the Trail of the Ancients.

Two scenic overlooks on the San Juan River, each a short drive from the highway, deserve a look, especially if you're recording your trip with photographs. **Goose-necks State Reserve** (three-quarters of a mile from where you turned onto UT 261, left 4 miles on a paved

road, $3 entrance fee) affords a close-up view of
1,500-foot-deep entrenched river meanders. Six miles
farther north, a 4-mile unpaved road on your left goes to
Muley Point, with a broader view of the river's labyrinth
and an interpretive display on the area's geology; free, no
facilities. Twenty-four miles north on UT 261 from the
Muley Point turnoff, you'll come to UT 95. Turn left
(west), and in less than a mile you'll reach the turnoff on
your right to Natural Bridges.

Natural Bridges National Monument

Tour Natural Bridges National Monument on the paved
8-mile scenic loop drive. The three natural bridges are
located in two adjacent canyons, with a hiking trail to
each one from the scenic loop. Owachomo Bridge is an
easy half-mile hike, while Sipapu and Kachina bridges are
each reached by a steep 1½-mile trail. Afternoon temperatures in the summer often reach 100 degrees, so if you'd
like to hike either of the longer trails, start early and plan
to complete your hike before noon. The monument also
has Anasazi cliff dwellings and pictographs. The visitors
center relies entirely on solar electricity. In 1980, when it
was built, it was the largest photovoltaic system on earth.

Travel Route: Natural Bridges to Moab (108 miles)

Drive east from Natural Bridges on UT 95 a distance of 32
miles to Blanding. Along the way, a well-marked half-mile
dirt road to the right (south) goes to Cave Towers, seven
Anasazi fortress towers used in the eleventh and twelfth
centuries to defend a permanent underground spring in a
cave below. If you are driving a low-clearance vehicle, the
best plan for seeing this ruin is to park near the highway
and walk up the dirt road, about an hour round-trip.
There is also a short hiking trail to Indian ruins from the
Butler Wash rest area. The easy 1-mile, half-hour
round-trip trail goes to an overlook from which numerous ruins can be seen. Join US 191 northbound (left) into
Blanding. Just south of town, 2⅓ miles from the junction, a paved access road on the left goes to Westwater

Ruin, yet another cliff dwelling. If you dare, cross West-water Canyon on the swinging bridge to see a small natural bridge.

In Blanding, **Edge of the Cedars State Historical Monument** has a group of small pueblos and kivas, some dating back to A.D. 700. The ruins themselves are not outstanding, but the museum is. Admission is $3.

Continue north from Blanding on US 191. Four miles north is **Devil's Canyon Campground**, a good picnic stop. Drive all the way to the end of the campground, where you'll find a short (400 yard) trail to the rim of a canyon that thwarted pioneers and road builders for generations. It's 21 miles from Blanding to the town of Monticello, 55 more miles to Moab, all scenic. Fifteen miles before Moab, on the right, is the improbable **Hole n'' the Rock Home**, a 5,000-square-foot dwelling carved into the red sandstone cliff by the late Albert and Gladys Christensen between 1945 and 1957, still run by their family as a gift and rock shop. If the stone bust of Franklin D. Roosevelt that Albert carved into the cliff face intrigues you, tour the home and see 14 rooms arranged around large pillars. The fireplace has a 65-foot chimney drilled through solid rock.

Moab

Moab (pop. 5,000) was a boomtown in the 1950s, when uranium prospecting along the Colorado River was big business. While other uranium towns have practically vanished from the map, Moab has flourished as a tourist town thanks to two new national parks nearby, Arches and Canyonlands. This is the place to fill up on gas and stock up on food and water.

During July and August, early afternoon in both Arches and Canyonlands is likely to be very hot. It's best to drive out to Canyonlands late in the afternoon, when you won't have to wait long for evening's coolness. In the meantime, you might drive the 60-mile **LaSal Mountain Loop** into cool mountain forests. Go north from Moab on US 191 and turn right onto UT 128 just before the bridge. Follow the Colorado River along the boundary of Arches National Park for 16 miles and take the turnoff to Castle Valley. Go south through Castle Valley 11 miles to the LaSal Mountain Loop Road turnoff on your right, which takes you into the national forest. The loop road will eventually bring you back to US 191 south of Moab. All but one mile of the route is paved.

If you are visiting the area during the cooler fall or spring months, skip the mountains and spend the afternoon seeing Arches National Park or arrive earlier at Canyonlands.

Canyonlands National Park: Island in the Sky

Be sure you have plenty of gas, food, and water before leaving Moab.

The turnoff to Island in the Sky is to the left off US 191, about 11 miles northwest of Moab, 6 miles past the Arches National Park turnoff. It's 22 miles from the highway to the park entrance. Stop and check in at the ranger station/visitors center, just past The Neck, a ridge no wider than the road, which is the only way on or off the "island."

Stewart Udall, President Kennedy's Secretary of the Interior, was surveying the site of a proposed dam on the Colorado River above Cataract Canyon from a small plane when he exclaimed, "My God, that's a national park down there!" Two years later, in 1964, Canyonlands National Park became a reality. If your idea of a national park is the Grand Canyon, Yellowstone, or Yosemite, the visitors center (in a converted mobile home) should tip you off that Canyonlands is different. Its 337,570 acres, sliced in thirds by the confluence of the Colorado and Green rivers, contain some of the least accessible land known to man. Most can only be reached by horseback, raft, or four-wheel drive; some can't be reached at all.

Island in the Sky is a long, narrow promontory between the two rivers, rising 2,000 feet above them. The recently paved roads fork at Green River Overlook, 7 miles past the entrance, and go to opposite ends of the

12-mile-long "island." At the south tip, **Grandview Point** affords a "look but don't touch" view from the exact center of Canyonlands National Park. Explore with binoculars and let your imagination roam over the marvelously complex landscape.

The White Rim is 1,000 feet below, midway down to river level. Look carefully and you may spot desert bighorn sheep grazing there. A four-wheel-drive road, the Shafer Trail, follows the White Rim all the way around the Island in the Sky. Almost due east is Monument Basin, with its white-capped red rock fins and spires. In the distance to the east (left) of the Colorado River is the Needles District, where most of the park's long-distance wilderness hiking trails are located. On the opposite side of the Green River, to the southwest, is The Maze. The far rim of The Maze is accessible only by an 80-mile four-wheel-drive road; in The Maze itself there are no developed trails. South as far as you can see, beyond the river junction, the Colorado disappears into Cataract Canyon, which many river rafters and kayakers consider the ultimate challenge in North America. A member of John Wesley Powell's 1869 Colorado River exploration team likened a boat trip down Cataract Canyon to riding "on the back of the dragon." Beyond Cataract Canyon is an area known simply as Ernie's Country. No road goes there.

There are few developed trails in this district of Canyonlands. The best hiking is in the area of **Upheaval Dome**, the crater of a collapsed salt dome. Two easy trails, each a one-mile, half-hour walk, leave from the Dome Road near the picnic area. Upheaval Dome Trail goes to the rim of the dome, with views into the center of the crater. Whale Rock Trail takes you to the top of a butte to view the dome from a distance. You can enjoy a longer hike along the Canyonlands rim from any of the overlooks, following the unofficial tracks of past hikers. Stay on the bare slickrock surfaces, away from vegetation; that way you won't disturb the fragile soil layer, and rattlesnakes won't disturb you.

Camping

The park's primitive 13-site campground is near Green River Overlook, 7 miles in from the visitors center. There are rest rooms but no water. Camping is free. The campground may be full by 6:00 p.m.

On the off-chance that the campground at Island in the Sky may be full when you arrive, go back outside the park boundary to the 7-mile paved side road to **Dead Horse Point State Park**, where you'll find a campground with all facilities and well-developed rim trails overlooking the Colorado River Canyon. Camping costs $8 (including the $3 entrance fee), so this campground fills up less often than the free one in Canyonlands. Another alternative is to spend the night at **Arches National Park** (see Day 11) and hike the Devil's Garden in the hours before dark or after dawn.

Lodging

Moab has a good selection of moderately priced accommodations. Chain motels such as the **Best Western Greenwell Motel**, 105 S. Main, (801) 259-6151, the **Ramada Inn**, 182 S. Main, (801) 259-7141, and the **Travelodge**, 550 S. Main, (801) 259-6171, cost from $45 to $55 double. Independent motels charge less. The **Kokopelli Lodge**, 72 S. First East, (901) 259-7615, offers newly remodeled rooms at $35 to $45. In the $25-$35 range, try the **Canyonlands Motel**, Main and Center Street, (801) 259-5167.

Moab's bed and breakfasts are small, so reservations should be made in advance. **Cedar Breaks Bed & Breakfast**, Center and Fourth East, (801) 259-7830, offers deluxe lodging in individual condos with kitchens, living rooms, and separate bedrooms, full breakfast included, for $55 double. The **Westwood Guest House**, 81 E. First South, (801)-259-7283, has three-room suites with kitchens and queen-size beds for $35 to $45 a night.

Food

Moab is the place to stock up on groceries. There are
three downtown supermarkets; you won't see another
one until you reach Kanab, Utah, three days from now.

Sixteen kinds of sandwiches, daily lunch and dinner
specials, and breakfast anytime are served at **The
Westerner**, 331 N. Main. This self-proclaimed historic
landmark diner dates back to the 1950s uranium boom,
when the original section was a "Wichita special"—a
trailer towed to Moab to feed hordes of hungry
prospectors.

ARCHES TO CAPITOL REEF

Today holds what may be a once-in-a-lifetime experience: three national parks in the same day. Awaken in Canyonlands and get an early start to tour Arches. Drive during the middle of the day, with a possible stop at Goblin Valley if the weather isn't too hot, and arrive at Capitol Reef in time to enjoy the cool of the evening in the least known of Utah's national parks.

Suggested Schedule

7:30 a.m.	Drive to Arches National Park.
8:00 a.m.	See Arches, hike.
12:00 noon	Drive to Green River.
1:30 p.m.	Drive to Goblin Valley.
2:30 p.m.	See Goblin Valley.
3:30 p.m.	Drive to Capitol Reef. Camp there or spend the night in nearby Torrey, Bicknell, or Loa.

Arches National Park

Arches is almost adjacent to Canyonlands. To get there, retrace your route from Island in the Sky to US 191 and go 6 miles east (back toward Moab) to the Arches National Park entrance.

Readers of *Desert Solitaire*, the late Edward Abbey's memoir of a season as a ranger in the small, almost inaccessible Arches National Monument in the 1950s, will recall his tirade against "national parkification" and, understandably, brace themselves for a bad case of too many tourists. In reality, it's not that bad. There is traffic on the park's paved roads, and the park service has put up signs telling you the names of all the major rock formations, but it's hardly Disneyland. Arrive as early in the morning as possible to beat both the heat and the press of other tourists.

Arches National Park, more than half of which is bare

rock, centers around a collapsed salt dome similar to Canyonlands' Upheaval Dome but larger. Salt deposits from ancient seas floated up to form a large underground deposit that fractured surface layers of sandstone, then groundwater dissolved the salt and washed it away. The dome collapsed, leaving a rim of fin formations, which freezing and thawing carved to make natural arches. The park has more natural arches than any other place in the world.

You can't appreciate Arches from behind a steering wheel. In fact, you can drive every road in the park and never understand its attraction. This is hiking country, with ten outstanding trails. The hike that will show you the most in a half-day visit is the **Devil's Garden Trail** from the campground at the end of the 21-mile main road. This moderate 5-mile loop trail leads to seven arches, including Landscape Arch, the world's longest natural span. It is the most popular trail in the park. For more remote hiking, turn off the main road on the unpaved road to Wolfe Ranch. At the old ranch cabin, you'll find the trailhead for **Delicate Arch Trail**, a steep 3-mile round-trip to perhaps the park's most beautiful arch. Allow three to four hours for either hike.

Travel Route: Arches to Capitol Reef (171 miles)

From the Arches National Park entrance, turn right (northwest) on US 191 and go 26 miles to Crescent Junction. Take I-70 westbound for 20 miles to Green River. **Green River State Park**, on the outskirts of town, has expansive green lawns and shade trees, a cool and pleasant picnic spot that could be worth the $3/day use fee.

Eleven miles west of Green River, exit the interstate southbound on UT Highway 24 to Hanksville, a distance of 51 miles. At 30 miles, you'll see a large sign on the right to **Goblin Valley State Park.** If you have time, take the 11-mile (last 6 unpaved) road into the park. There is a $3/day use fee. Goblin Valley's weird rock formations are unlike any other weird rock formations you've seen: imagine giant petrified milk chocolate-covered Walt Dis-

Southwestern Utah

ney mushrooms, set against a backdrop of buttes eroded to resemble Mayan pyramids. If you can imagine that, you'll love this place. It may be too hot to walk through the valley in midafternoon. If you'd like to spend the night here and see it in the early evening but don't want to pay the $8 camping fee (there's no water anyway), camp free around the other side of the butte on the Wild Horse Butte road, which branches off just before the park entrance.

From Hanksville, continuing on UT 24, it's 30 miles to the entrance of Capitol Reef National Park.

Capitol Reef National Park

Capitol Reef may be the national park system's best-kept secret. Established in 1971, it remains the least visited of Utah's national parks. Besides offering a variety of short and long hiking trails, unpaved auto roads, four-wheel-drive roads, and trackless wilderness, the park protects ancient petroglyphs, a well-preserved Mormon pioneer village, and orchards where visitors can pick fruit right off the trees.

The park's most visible points of interest, listed in order below, cluster along UT 24 on the 9-mile drive up the Fremont River from the entrance gate to the visitors center and campground. Take your time. Tomorrow morning you'll have a chance to sample the park's back-country.

Sightseeing Highlights

▲ **Behunin Cabin**—Elijah Behunin, the area's first set-tler (1882), lived with his wife and ten children in this stone cabin, which was smaller than most modern camp-ing vehicles. The next time you have to huddle in your rig or tent until the rain stops, think of Elijah.

▲ **Hickman Bridge**—A one-mile (each way) trail climbs switchbacks 380 feet through a small canyon and under the 133-foot natural bridge. Along the way are Indian ruins and fine views of white-capped domes, including Capitol Dome, for which the "reef" (uplifted cliff) is named. Allow two hours for the hike.

▲▲ **Petroglyphs**—Fremont Indians, who lived here at least as early as A.D. 800, left this rock art for us to admire. Experts do not know its meaning; do you? The best petroglyphs are reached on a short, easy trail from the parking pullout.

▲ **Fruita Schoolhouse**—This country school served the pioneer community of Fruita (originally named "The Eden of Wayne County"), where the visitors center and campground are now located. The school, used from 1896 to 1941, is the only building left standing.

▲▲ **Orchards**—While no houses remain from old Fruita, the 2,500 cherry, apple, peach, and apricot trees that were the village's lifeblood endure, preserved by the National Park Service as a Historic Landscape. Pruning, irrigation, and replanting are done by park service employees. When the fruit ripens, the public is invited to pick it, then pay the park service the same price per pound that local orchards get. Harvest dates are posted at the visitors center.

▲▲ **Fremont River Trail**—An easy walk upriver from the campground through the orchards will bring you to the trail, which follows the riverbank for half a mile. If you're feeling adventurous and have at least 2½ hours, stay on the trail for the steep climb—800 feet in three-quarters of a mile—up Miner's Peak for a fine view of Fruita and the reef.

▲▲ **Cohab Canyon Trail**—Starting just across the road from the campground, this trail climbs a quarter-mile by switchbacks to a slickrock canyon, goes almost 2 miles through the canyon, and comes out at the river across the road from the Hickman Bridge trailhead. (Cohab Canyon and Hickman Bridge trails can be combined for a great all-morning hike.) The canyon got its name because, so the story goes, Mormon "cohabitationists" used it to hide out from U.S. marshals trying to enforce the federal law against polygamy.

Camping

Fruita Campground at Capitol Reef National Park is the only federal campground in the Southwest with a green lawn at each campsite. It is on the riverbank, surrounded by orchards, with two trails (described above) for evening or morning walks; $5 per night. Nightly naturalist slide shows are presented at the campground amphitheater from May through September.

If you're traveling in July or August, and you arrive after 6:00 p.m., you may find the Capitol Reef campground full. There are three national forest campgrounds higher in the mountains, within 20 miles southeast of Torrey on UT 12. The first, **Singletree**, offers a good view of the valley and beyond to the Henry Mountains, the last place in the lower 48 United States to be explored and mapped. **Pleasant Creek** and neighboring **Oak Creek** campgrounds are said to have marauding skunks (*"Thousands of skunks!"* according to the campground host). Stash all food inside your vehicle at night.

Lodging

This national park has no lodge. You'll find a few motels, as well as restaurants and service stations, in the towns of Torrey (11 miles from the visitors center on US 24), Bicknell (19 miles), and Loa (26 miles).

CAPITOL REEF TO BRYCE CANYON

The drive from Capitol Reef to Bryce Canyon, by way of Escalante Canyons, is among the most beautiful stretches of road on this tour. Bryce Canyon is congested with tourist traffic, but the scenery is worth braving the masses for. Test your crowd-avoiding strategy (which will also work at the Grand Canyon) by taking an easy walk along the canyon rim or a more demanding one down among the hoodoos.

Suggested Schedule

9:00 a.m.	Capitol Reef Scenic Drive and/or hike.
12:00 noon	Drive to Escalante Canyons.
1:00 p.m.	Picnic.
2:00 p.m.	Drive to Bryce Canyon.
3:00 p.m.	Get campsite (or check into lodge).
3:30 p.m.	See Bryce Canyon National Park.

Capitol Reef Scenic Drive

Spend the morning hiking in Capitol Reef or take the 8-mile unpaved Scenic Drive south from the visitors center. Take time to look at the gigantic 3-D relief map in the visitors center first. A self-guided tour brochure, available free at the visitors center, explains the area's geology.

The last 2 miles of the Scenic Drive were once (from 1884 to 1962) part of the main "highway" through south-central Utah. Beyond the end of the Scenic Drive, the old road continues as Capitol Gorge Trail. An easy 2-mile round-trip hike takes you to Indian petroglyphs, a pioneer register, and The Tanks—pockets in the rock which capture rainwater pools, hence the other name for the Capitol Reef formation, Waterpocket Fold. Butch Cassidy, for years a hero in these parts as he robbed from the rich (plundering trains and banks all over the Four Corners region) and shared with the poor (including not only his gang members but also local folks who guarded the secret of his whereabouts), frequently used this route to reach his hideout nearby.

The scenic drive is not a loop. Drive back to the visitors center the same way you came.

Travel Route: Capitol Reef to Bryce Canyon (104 miles)

Drive west from Capitol Reef on UT 24 for 11 miles. As you near the town of Torrey, turn left (south) on UT 12 and stay on that highway all the way to Bryce Canyon National Park. The first 33 miles of the route climb into Dixie National Forest, through ponderosa forest between Boulder Mountain and Impossible Peak, and descend into the town of Boulder, where Anasazi Indian Village State Park is located.

From there, the highway descends into **Escalante Canyons**, a Bureau of Land Management Scenic Area. If the U.S. government ever decides southern Utah needs a sixth national park, this area and the adjoining Box-Death Hollow Wilderness will be the prime candidate. Until then, it's our secret. The best picnic stop-and-walk is Calf Creek Recreation Area, on your right about a mile before the bottom of the canyon, where a 2-mile trail leads past two Anasazi village ruins to Calf Creek Falls. Beyond the canyons, 18 miles from Boulder, is the town of Escalante. The local attraction is **Escalante Petrified Forest State Park** ($3 entrance fee), which also has cliff dwellings. Forty-two more miles across grazing land will bring you to the entrance of Bryce Canyon National Park.

Bryce Canyon National Park

Brace yourself for Bryce Canyon, a victim of its own success. Anytime between Memorial Day and Labor Day, it will be crowded. Bryce Canyon (formerly Utah National Monument) became a national park in 1923, just four years after the Grand Canyon did. Its proximity to the Grand Canyon makes it an ideal stop on loop tours that take in the North Rim, Zion, and Glen Canyon Dam. Many times more tourists visit Bryce Canyon than Island in the Sky, Arches, and Capitol Reef combined. The 18-mile paved drive through the park has traffic at all times, and the scenic overlook pullouts are about as much fun as a shopping mall parking lot.

Fortunately, there's a way to beat the crowds at Bryce: walk. Few visitors do, though the park has 60 miles of beautifully maintained trails. I suggest you skip the drive to the far end of the park. The most spectacular formations can be seen on the easy **Rim Trail** that runs 6 miles from Fairyland View to Sunset Point, Sunrise Point, and finally Bryce Point. Take part or all of it. A shuttle service is available for one-way hikes. More ambitious hikers with at least five hours to spend can get down among the hoodoos on the strenuous 5 ½ -mile **Fairyland Loop Trail**, which also runs between Sunrise Point and Fairyland View, then take the shuttle back or walk back along the Rim Trail for a good view of where they've been.

The eroded shale-and-sandstone uplifts of Bryce Canyon are absolutely unique. The park service even invented a new name for the white and bright orange obelisks and spires: "hoodoo," which they define as "a pinnacle, pillar, or odd-shaped rock left standing by the forces of erosion." Bryce Canyon, by the way, was named after Ebenezer Bryce, a homesteader who tried to graze cattle here between 1875 and 1880. Bryce's opinion of the scenery was, "It's a hell of a place to lose a cow."

Camping
Bryce Canyon has two campgrounds, **North Campground** and **Sunset Campground**. Together they have 218 campsites, with separate loops for RVs and tent campers. By around 5:00 p.m., the campsite registration areas will be a traffic jam of campers and motor homes. Stake your claim to a campsite as soon as you arrive in the park and sightsee afterward. Both campgrounds have campfire programs. Campsites cost $7. Pay showers and laundry facilities, as well as pay telephones, are available at the Sunrise Point Camper Store.

Lodging

For a roof over your head, you can do no better than a room or cabin at **Bryce Lodge**, (801) 834-5361, in the park. The rustic elegance is a bargain in the $60-$70 price range. Reservations are a must. Main lodge units have two queen-size beds, full bath, and private porch. The carpeted cabins have fireplaces.

Other accommodations near the park entrance include **Best Western Ruby's Inn**, (801) 834-7686; **Bryce Canyon Pines**, (801) 834-5336; and **Pink Cliffs Village**, (801) 834-5303. There are also motels in nearby towns. Expect to pay tourist zone prices, $45-$70, at any of these places.

Food

Fine dining can be found at the **Bryce Lodge** dining room. Groceries are sold at the **Camper Store** nearby.

GLEN CANYON DAM AND LEE'S FERRY

After a leisurely, slow-to-get-going morning at Bryce Canyon, drive down to the Colorado River. You saw it on Day 10 from Island in the Sky, and you'll see it again tomorrow from the rim of the Grand Canyon. Today, you'll see the river in two of its other aspects: from the top of its largest dam and, just a few miles downriver, from the exact spot where the Grand Canyon begins.

Suggested Schedule

9:00 a.m.	Take a hike at Bryce Canyon.
11:00 a.m.	Drive from Bryce Canyon to Kanab. Lunch there.
1:30 p.m.	Drive to Glen Canyon Dam.
3:00 p.m.	Take the dam tour.
4:30 p.m.	Drive to Lee's Ferry.
5:30 p.m.	Camp at Lee's Ferry.

Travel Route: Bryce Canyon to Lee's Ferry (126 miles)

Leaving Bryce Canyon, take UT 12 westbound, 13 miles through Red Canyon to the intersection with US 89. From here on, it's impossible to get lost. Just follow the big green-and-white "Grand Canyon" signs. Turn south (left) on US 89 and stay on it all the way to Kanab, 61 miles. Along the way, watch on your left for the privately operated Moqui Cave. If you like caves, here's one; but the real attraction is the entrance in the shape of a triceratops—a classic bit of tourist kitsch.

There's a supermarket in Kanab, in case you're low on provisions by now. From Kanab, stay on US 89 to Lake Powell. The driving distance to Glen Canyon Dam is 85 miles.

After touring the dam, continue south for 23 more miles, across the corner of the Navajo Reservation, to Bitter Springs, where Alternate US 89 turns north (right) to

Marble Canyon. Another 14 miles will bring you to
Navajo Bridge, the first bridge across the Colorado River
when it was built in the 1920s. Just past the village of Marble Canyon, follow the 4-mile road on your right (north)
to Lee's Ferry, Glen Canyon National Recreation Area.

Sightseeing Highlights
▲▲ Glen Canyon Dam—The northernmost and largest
of the dams that form the Colorado River Project (the
other major ones are Hoover Dam on Lake Mead, Davis
Dam on Lake Mojave, and Parker Dam on Lake Havasu),
Glen Canyon Dam generates unimaginable amounts of
electricity and sends it by power lines straight across 600
miles of desert to southern California. Take the guided
tour into the bowels of the dam to see the water turbines
and the long row of transformers, each of which pours
out 345,000 volts of electricity.

Environmentalists have never forgiven the government
for building this dam, which flooded one of the last
unexplored areas in the United States. It may seem
strange that, with all this water and energy, the surrounding land is arid and empty. Virtually none of the water in
the Colorado River or its reservoirs is used for irrigation
until it reaches southern California. About one-third of
the river's water evaporates from the lake surfaces. What
remains is diverted by pipeline just north of the Mexican
border to irrigate the Imperial Valley. Glen Canyon Dam
traps Colorado River silt, sand, and mining wastes, filling
up the lakebed several feet each year. In less than two
centuries, experts say, Lake Powell will be a vast barren
mud flat, while the dam, its generators rusted and silent,
will be one of the world's largest man-made waterfalls.
(Powell Falls National Monument? Squint your eyes and
you can almost see it.)

The visitors center is open daily from 7:00 a.m. to 7:00
p.m. during the summer months and 8:30 a.m. to 5:30
p.m. the rest of the year.

Change your watch when you cross the dam. Arizona
does not change to daylight saving time, as other south-

western states do. Most Arizonans live in the hot climate of Phoenix and Tucson, where they prefer long cool summer evenings, not more daylight. When it's 3:00 p.m. on the Utah side of the dam, it's 4:00 p.m. on the Arizona side.

▲ **John Wesley Powell Museum**—This free museum at Lake Powell Boulevard and Navajo Drive in Page, about 2 miles past the dam on the Arizona side, recounts the adventures of the man who led the first expedition down the Colorado River through Cataract Canyon and the Grand Canyon (1869), braving the white water in wooden boats. There are also Indian artifacts and exhibits that explain the geology of the river and its canyons. The museum is open weekdays from 8:00 a.m. to 6:00 p.m., Tuesdays until 8:00 p.m., and Sundays from 10:00 a.m. to 6:00 p.m., closed Saturdays, during the summer months; in the spring and October, it closes at 5:00 p.m. and is not open on weekends; closed during the winter months. Admission is free.

▲ **Lee's Ferry**—John D. Lee established the first ferry across the Colorado River here in Marble Canyon in 1871. He was a fugitive at the time for leading fellow Mormons to massacre a wagon train of California-bound pioneers. He came here to hide, went into business, and lived here with one of his 17 wives until U.S. marshals found him and shot him.

Lee's Ferry is still the only road to river level on the Colorado between Green River, Utah, and the California state line, a distance of over 600 river miles. Though just a few miles downriver from Glen Canyon Dam, here in Marble Canyon you'll find rare, wild beauty barely touched by mankind. Lee's Ferry is the departure point for all white-water rafting and kayaking expeditions into the Grand Canyon. You can watch them set out any morning from the launch ramp at the end of the road.

On the river, across the main road from the campground, is a long sandy beach, the easiest water access for area wildlife and the only place you're likely to spot a beaver in the desert. Temperatures by the river are much cooler than at the campground. As you bask on the beach, notice the narrow strip of white limestone that rises diagonally out of the water on the cliffs across the river. Here is where the Grand Canyon begins: the white layer keeps slanting upward to become the surface of the Kaibab Plateau, the rim of the Grand Canyon.

Camping
Lee's Ferry Campground has rest rooms, water, and picnic tables with shade roofs. Used primarily by fishermen, the campground is crowded on weekends but practically empty during the week. There are no hookups. The camping fee is $6.

Lodging
Page (pop. 6,500), on the Arizona side of Glen Canyon Dam, has a handful of motor inns that cater primarily to boating enthusiasts, such as the **Holiday Inn/Lake Powell** (287 N. Lake Powell Boulevard, 602-645-8851, $75 to $85 double) and the **Inn at Lake Powell** (formerly a Ramada Inn, 716 Rim View Drive, 602-645-2466, $62 to $75 double).

Itinerary Option
For information on all-day boat excursions from Glen Canyon Dam to Rainbow Bridge National Monument, 50 miles northwest and only accessible by water, contact the Superintendent, Glen Canyon National Recreation Area, Box 1507, Page, AZ 86040, (602) 645-2471. To arrange boat rentals or charters and find out about privately operated tours, call Wahweap Marina, (602) 645-2433.

THE GRAND CANYON: NORTH RIM

The North Rim of the Grand Canyon is a thousand feet higher than the South Rim—8,255 feet above sea level and about 4,300 feet above the Colorado River in the bottom of the canyon. Some people contend that the view is better from the South Rim, because you can see the river from there. I like the North Rim view just fine, the climate is cooler, and this side of the canyon is less visited and less extensively developed.

Suggested Schedule

8:30 a.m.	Drive to Jacob Lake.
10:00 a.m.	Drive to Grand Canyon North Rim.
12:00 noon	Arrive at North Rim. Get a campsite or check into the lodge.
1:00 p.m.	Relax on a gentle walk along the Transept Trail to the lodge and out to Bright Angel Point.
Evening	Dine in or out. Catch the campfire talk or join a night sky walk to Bright Angel Point.

Travel Route: Lee's Ferry to Grand Canyon North Rim (83 miles)

Get an early start. The Grand Canyon North Rim campground sometimes fills up by noon.

A 41-mile drive west on US 89 Alternate will take you up through the ponderosa pine forests of the Kaibab Plateau to Jacob Lake. Turn south on AZ 67. Near the intersection, you'll see a park service portable building by the side of the road. Stop for information on campsite availability at the Grand Canyon. If there is any problem, the rangers will direct you to alternate campgrounds in the national forest.

From Jacob Lake, it's 42 more miles on AZ 67 to the North Rim. Admission to the Grand Canyon is $5 per

Grand Canyon

vehicle. Be sure to save your receipt; it is valid for 7 days and will also get you into the South Rim (Day 19).

The Grand Canyon

Even at the Grand Canyon, one of the nation's most popular parks, you can find solitude by hiking one of the trails that lead to more isolated points along the rim. Some are longer than others, but all are level and easy to walk.

The popular **Transept Trail** leads 1½ miles from the campground to the lodge along the canyon rim. An extension of the trail from the lodge goes another quarter-mile to Bright Angel Point. Take this walk as soon as you've arranged your campsite or lodging, and think, "Wow! The Grand Canyon!"

A longer and less-frequented route is the **Uncle Jim Trail**, which starts from the North Kaibab Trailhead. From the campground, cross the main road and follow the path around the water tanks; when you reach the road again, you're there. Follow the trail that goes back into the woods, not the one that goes down into the canyon. It is a 5-mile round-trip walk to Uncle Jim Point (named for Jim Owens, the warden of Grand Canyon Game Preserve until it became a national park in 1919). Allow three hours for the walk.

The **Ken Patrick Trail** branches to the left from Uncle Jim Trail 1 mile along, and goes another 10 miles (one way) to **Point Imperial**. The hike takes six hours each way. It goes deep into the forest but only affords canyon views around Point Imperial, to which you can also drive. The most practical plan for hiking this trail is to drive to Point Imperial and walk partway back along the trail, or arrange for someone less athletic than you to drive out there in six hours and pick you up.

Perhaps the most enjoyable rim walk in the park is the **Widforss Trail**. The trailhead is 1 mile in on a dirt road that leaves the main road 1¼ miles from the campground, one-quarter mile from the Cape Royal Road junction. This 10-mile round-trip (allow five hours) skirts the Transept rim, then takes you into the forest and brings you back to the rim overlooking Haunted Canyon. There is a picnic area at Widforss Point (named for Gunnar Widforss, a Swedish artist who made a career of painting America's national parks in the 1920s).

It is not possible to hike to the bottom of the Grand Canyon and back the same day. You can hike partway down the **North Kaibab Trail**, but be warned: the first part of the trail is the steepest, dropping 2,000 feet in not much more than a mile. Climbing back up will take four times as long as going down. An all-day, 9½-mile round-trip hike to the swimming holes near where Roaring Springs Canyon joins Bright Angel Creek will make you feel like you've hiked the Grand Canyon.

Camping
North Rim Campground, perched practically on the edge of the Grand Canyon, has 86 campsites, first-come, first-served. The campground has a laundromat and

coin-operated showers. This is not a large campground for such a popular area. In fact, the North Rim has only about one-third the campground capacity of Bryce Canyon. If the campground is full, as it may well be if you arrive later than noon, the rangers at the Jacob Lake information booth will point you toward another campground in the national forest and tell you what time to line up if you want a North Rim campsite tomorrow. To assure a campsite at the rim, you can make reservations (at least a month in advance) by mail through TICKETRON Reservation Office, 401 Hackensack Avenue, Hackensack, NJ 07601, or by calling (602) 340-9033 or (213) 410-1720 with your Visa or MasterCard in hand. Camping fees start at $10.

Lodging
North Rim Lodge, the only accommodation within the park, offers modern guest rooms as well as three types of individual cabins. Prices range between $46 and $62 double. Make reservations well in advance through TWA Services, (801) 586-7686.

Slightly lower-cost accommodations, with a pleasant forest setting but no canyon view, can be found at **Jacob Lake Inn**, (602) 643-7232. Rates range from about $40 to $55.

Food
The dining room at the **North Rim Lodge**, with its panoramic picture window view, serves a limited selection of fine food at moderate prices, breakfast, lunch, and dinner. Reservations are essential for dinner; go to the lodge and make them in person. Breakfast overlooking the Grand Canyon is an experience to remember.

Itinerary Option: Toroweap Point
If solitude is what you crave and a 140-mile drive on unpaved roads doesn't intimidate you, allow an extra day in your itinerary for a drive out to Toroweap Point at the west end of the canyon, where you can be alone on the rim for a more personal Grand Canyon experience.

This route involves driving on unpaved roads for 67 miles to Toroweap Point today and another 67 (or more) unpaved miles back out tomorrow. The roads are wide and well graded—better, in fact, than some paved highways you've driven on the Navajo Reservation—but there is no gas, food, or water anywhere. Nobody lives out here. If your vehicle breaks down and you can't fix it, you may have a long wait before anyone comes along and can fetch help, so carry twice as much food and water as you think you'll need. Don't try this trip if thunderstorms threaten: flash floods are possible, and the road can be slippery when wet. Storms occur in the afternoon, almost never in the morning, so if you can get there, you can count on being able to get back.

From the North Rim, retrace your route to Jacob Lake and Fredonia, a distance of 75 miles. At Fredonia, turn west (left) on AZ 389 and go 15 miles to **Pipe Springs National Monument** on the Kaibab Paiute Indian Reservation. Around the 9-mile point on the way, watch for the unpaved road that goes south. This is the road you'll want to take after seeing Pipe Springs.

A well-preserved remnant of Mormon pioneer life, the ranch that is now Pipe Springs National Monument was established to graze cattle tithed to the church by ranchers throughout the Arizona Strip. The founder's name was Winsor so, naturally enough, the fortresslike stone main house bears the nickname, "Winsor Castle." As the only telegraph station in the Strip, the ranch became a communications center. Women from the historical society in Fredonia, wearing authentic period dress, demonstrate weaving, quilting, and other pioneer crafts in the castle's antique-furnished rooms. Open 8:00 a.m. to 5:00 p.m.

The drive to Toroweap Point takes you across the **Arizona Strip** (no relation to the Las Vegas Strip). Pioneer ranchers discovered the area in the 1870s, at a time when there were several years of exceptional rainfall. Thinking they'd discovered a cattleman's paradise, they moved large beef herds into the area. Then the rain stopped. The cattle overgrazed the sparse vegetation, then starved. Today a handful of Paiute and Anglo ranchers run a few cattle over the vast area, but you're more likely to see pronghorn antelope.

The signs on the road to Toroweap are confusing. The inconspicuous sign at the highway turnoff says the road goes to Mt. Trumbull. Follow signs to "Tuweap," "Toroweap," or "Grand Canyon National Monument" whenever you see them, but pay no attention to the distances posted, which are wildly contradictory. Otherwise, just stay on what looks like the most-used road at each fork and maintain a southerly direction. A three-hour drive (60 miles) across the Arizona Strip will bring you to the Grand Canyon National Park boundary fence. There is a house near the entrancececeherere park ranger used to live, but it apparently hasn't been occupied in some time. The last 7 miles to the rim are bumpier. The informal campground is all the way at the end of the road, on the very tip of Toroweap Point.

Toroweap Point is the Grand Canyon's "back door," a wilderness area that hardly anyone sees. The last time I was there, on a Saturday afternoon in the middle of the tourist season, the only other visitors were a painter and a photographer. On weekdays you may find yourself completely alone on the canyon rim.

The rim here is lower than in the main part of the park. The approach to Toroweap Point is through a notch in the upper rim, so the point is actually on the hot, dry slickrock inner rim, the one you overlook from the North Rim, and about 100 miles downriver. The Colorado River is nearly 2,000 feet below you, between sheer cliffs. You can watch tiny-looking river rafts as they float past. The silence and the canyon's acoustics actually make it possible to eavesdrop on rafters' conversations. Toroweap Point also affords the only view of a major Grand Canyon formation, Vulcan's Throne.

When you leave Toroweap Point, instead of backtracking to rejoin the main itinerary at Fredonia, you can take a different unpaved road across the Arizona Strip to rejoin the main 22-day itinerary at St. George. The shortcut is 97 miles, all unpaved road, compared to 67 miles of unpaved road and 90 miles of highway. If you take the shortcut, you'll miss Zion National Park and save as much as an hour of driving time, depending on road conditions. To take this shortcut, backtrack 14 miles north from Toroweap Point, then take the road that forks to the left (west) to Mt. Trumbull. Twenty miles on, the road turns north. Stay on the same lonely road north for 63 more miles, and you'll suddenly come to St. George and I-15. Allow four to five hours for the drive.

ZION AND VALLEY OF FIRE

You can't cross the Grand Canyon by road. To get to the other side of the Colorado River, drive west beyond the end of the canyon, past Lake Mead, and across Hoover Dam. This route will bring you within a stone's throw of Las Vegas. Take time along the way to see Zion National Park and enjoy a warm desert night at the Valley of Fire, then enter the city tomorrow morning.

Suggested Schedule

8:30 a.m.	Breakfast at North Rim Lodge.
10:00 a.m.	Drive to Kanab.
12:00 noon	Drive to Zion National Park.
1:00 p.m.	Explore Zion.
3:30 p.m. or later	Zion to I-15 to Valley of Fire.
Evening	Camp at Valley of Fire, or stay in Las Vegas.

Travel Route: Grand Canyon via Zion to Valley of Fire (256 miles)

From the Grand Canyon North Rim, retrace your Day 14 route 75 miles north to Fredonia (where people returning from Toroweap Point rejoin the main route). Stay on US 89 for 17 more miles until you come to Mount Carmel Junction, then turn left on UT 9 to Zion National Park. Pay the $5 per vehicle fee.

From the entrance to Zion, it's 51 miles westbound on UT 9, through the town of Hurricane, to St. George, southwestern Utah's largest city (pop. 12,000), where you will join I-15 southbound. A long, scenic descent through the Virgin River Gorge will drop you into the Mojave Desert, the lowest elevation and hottest place on this tour route. Thirteen miles south on the interstate, you will cross into Arizona briefly; 26 more miles will bring you to the Nevada state line. Thirty miles into Nevada, at the Glendale exit, leave I-15, follow NV 169 nine miles

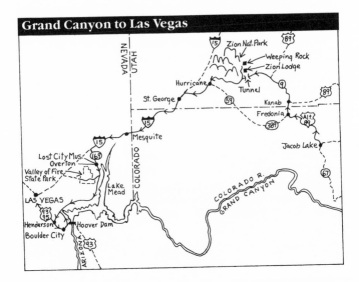

Grand Canyon to Las Vegas

past the town of Overton and take the road that turns
right (west) to Valley of Fire State Park.

If you'd like to get in out of the heat for a while, visit
Lost City Museum in Overton, a comprehensive exhibit
of the early Pueblo culture that thrived here around A.D.
800. Open daily until 4:30 p.m., free admission.

If you can't wait to get your hand on a slot machine
handle or your head under a roof (air-conditioned), simply stay on I-15 for one more hour and you'll find yourself in the middle of Las Vegas. Hop off the interstate at
Sahara Boulevard and go east a few blocks to Las Vegas
Boulevard South, better known as the Strip.

Sightseeing Highlights
▲▲ **Zion National Park**—When early Mormon settler
Isaac Behunin named this spectacular stretch of gorge Little Zion after the heavenly city of God, he was quite serious. "These great mountains," he declared, "are natural
temples of God. We can worship here as well as in the

man-made temples." Zion became a national park in
1918, a year before the Grand Canyon did.

Zion is the quintessential scenic drive, a brief but
intense burst of visual glory midway between the Grand
Canyon and Las Vegas. The main road, with its long tunnel, tantalizing peek-aboo windows, and sudden descent
into Zion Canyon, is worth the price of admission.

But people who don't get out of their cars can only
catch a too-brief glimpse of Zion's beauty. Start with the
short, easy walk to **Weeping Rock** from the parking area
just past the main lodge.

You have time to explore. It's only two hours from here
to your campground for the night, and if you arrive too
early, it will still be very hot. Though most Zion backcountry can only be reached on overnight hikes, any of
the following trails makes a reasonable half-day or less
hike: the **Emerald Pools Trail** starting at Zion Lodge, 1.2
miles round-trip; the **Hidden Canyon Trail** starting
from the Weeping Rock parking area, 2 miles round-trip;
the **Gateway to the Narrows Trail** starting at the Temple of Sinawava, 2 miles round-trip; the **Canyon Overlook Trail** starting from the tunnel overlook parking
area, 1 mile, steep; or the **Watchman Viewpoint Trail**
starting at the south campground, 2 miles round-trip,
steep. Carry plenty of water!

▲▲ **Valley of Fire State Park**—White and red sandstone layers have fractured and eroded into a bewildering
maze, best appreciated on a short hike into **Mouse's
Tank**, where an Indian renegade named Old Mouse and
about 50 followers hid out while raiding area ranches. It
took the cavalry 11 years to find them. Thousand-year-
old petroglyphs, scratched with wooden atlatls (spear-
throwing sticks) in the soft stone surfaces by nomadic
Indian hunters, decorate the walls of several canyons
within the park. Hiking is best soon after dawn, when
tracks of nighttime wildlife are fresh and the large white
nocturnal flowers of the sacred datura are still open. You
might even catch a rare glimpse of a desert bighorn sheep.

Camping
Valley of Fire State Park Campground has 38 camp-sites, picnic tables, and running water. Staying here enables you to explore the park early in the morning.

South along Lake Mead Drive, you'll find lakeside camping at **Overton Beach, Echo Bay**, and **Hemenway Beach**.

Lodging
Las Vegas is full of hotels. See the listings in Day 16.

Food
Buy any groceries you need in St. George. There is no food service at or near the Valley of Fire. See tomorrow's listings for dining in Las Vegas.

LAKE MEAD AND LAS VEGAS

Of all the subcultures that thrive in southwestern isolation—New Mexico's Norteños, the Mormons, and the various Native American groups—the newest and fastest growing is to be found in Las Vegas.

On this tour, you've seen example after dramatic example of nature in action. The nature you'll see in Las Vegas is human nature, the action takes seconds instead of centuries, and the wildlife feeds on casino chips. Think of it as Greed National Park and plunge deep into the air-conditioned fast-money clatter. But first, check out the countryside. While Las Vegas welcomes 13 million visitors each year, remarkably few leave the Strip or Glitter Gulch to see the varied and starkly beautiful landscapes that lie just outside of the city. Take time to drive the scenic route along the Lake Mead shore to Hoover Dam.

Suggested Schedule

8:00 a.m.	Explore Valley of Fire.
10:00 a.m.	Lake Mead drive.
12:30 p.m.	Hoover Dam to Las Vegas.
1:00 p.m.	Check into a casino hotel along the Strip.
1:30 p.m.	Clean up and cool off.
2:00 p.m.	Wander your hotel and those nearby, or visit a museum.
4:00 p.m.	Nap.
6:00 p.m.	Dinner.
Evening	Strip nightlife—stay out late.

Lake Mead Scenic Drive

After exploring the Valley of Fire early in the morning, exit the same way you came in. (If you continued in the same direction, out the park's other entrance, you'd come out on I-15, 33 miles north of the city.) Where the park road intersects the Lake Mead Scenic Drive, turn left (or continue straight for a brief stop at Overton Beach, 2 miles farther on, then return to the Lake Mead road).

The Lake Mead Scenic Drive parallels the shoreline for 42 miles, but for the first hour of the drive you won't see the lake from the road; instead, you'll follow dry Las Vegas Wash. Stop and let tiny tropical fish nibble your toes in **Rogers Warm Spring**, on your right. For a lake view, visit **Echo Bay**, two miles down a road on your left.

You know you're nearing the end of the Lake Mead road when you see often-lively **Hemenway Beach** and its campground. Stop and splash. The water's fine, though you'll want sandals because the beach is rocky. Warm and cold convection currents in the lake water tingle swimmers' skin. Use caution when wading: this is the rim of a flooded canyon, and not far from shore, submerged cliffs drop off into water 400 feet deep.

A few miles south of the beach, the road joins US 93. Turn left (east) and descend by switchbacks to **Hoover Dam**, the oldest dam on the Colorado River, completed in 1935. Tours ($1 per person) take you by elevator down through the center of the dam to the power plant, daily from 7:30 a.m. to 7:15 p.m. Memorial Day to Labor Day, 9:00 a.m. to 4:15 p.m. the rest of the year. See the large relief map of the Colorado River in the visitors center. Check out the dam's unusual art deco ornamentation, including winged sculptures called Figures of the Republic and a terrazzo representation of the solar system with astrological overtones.

Hoover Dam is also an impressive sight at night under lights. After dark, looking over the wall by the parking area on the Nevada side, you may see ringtail cats that inhabit the cliff, small elusive nocturnal desert cousins of the raccoon.

Leaving Hoover Dam the same way you came, stay on US 93 through Boulder City, which was the largest town in southern Nevada before World War II, and continue 23 miles to Las Vegas. US 93 is the city's eastern edge. To reach the Strip, turn left on Tropicana Road or Desert Inn Road. You can't miss it.

Las Vegas
Mormon pioneers tried to establish a fort settlement at Las Vegas ("The Meadows," named by a Mexican trading expedition scout) but failed. By 1864, when Nevada became a state, the area had no population at all. In 1931, when Nevada legalized gambling, Las Vegas was a small railroad and ranching town, seven blocks long, with a countywide population of 5,000.

El Rancho, the first casino resort on what is now the Strip, opened in 1941, but only after World War II, when Los Angeles (at a distance of 300 miles, the nearest city to Las Vegas) boomed, did casino development begin in earnest. In 1946, "Bugsy" Siegel built the lavish Flamingo, reputedly with organized crime backing. The rumor seemed to be confirmed when, six months later, Siegel was shot and killed by hit men in his Hollywood home. The Flamingo is now owned by the Hilton chain. Despite Las Vegas' gangster mystique, however, most casinos have never had any organized crime connections.

Today, Las Vegas has a population of over 500,000—more than half the population of the entire state of Nevada.

On payday in the Old West, cowboys would head for the nearest saloon town to drink, gamble, and chase fancy women. Las Vegas serves the same purpose as those old-time saloon towns but on a grand scale. Today's casinos play host to cowboys and oil riggers from all over the West as well as to millions of visitors who are neither. Old-timers, who are often heard to refer to the city as "Lost Wages," like to point out that "Vegas is where Americans come to do all the things they could do at home if they weren't so respectable."

To the north of Las Vegas is the U.S. Nuclear Testing Site. The first nuclear weapon atmospheric tests were conducted here in 1951, and each test became a local event as picnickers gathered to see the mushroom cloud 75 miles away. Six years later, the nuclear tests were moved underground, much to the disappointment of spectators.

Las Vegas' major sightseeing highlights are the casino hotels themselves. If gambling isn't your idea of fun, wander the maze of casinos anyway—you'll find all manner of garish marvels calculated to lure players away from the competition. You'll also see more money changing hands faster than you've ever imagined, amid a full range of human emotion from euphoria to despair: high drama that makes for world-class people-watching.

There are two casino districts. The Strip, on and near which all the major resort hotels are located, is Las Vegas Boulevard South, from the 2000 block (just north of Sahara Avenue) to the Hacienda at the 3900 block. Downtown casinos center on Fremont Street west of Las Vegas Boulevard, commonly known as Glitter Gulch. Fremont Street has some fine hotels, most notably the luxurious Union Plaza, as well as small sleazy casinos where hucksters lure players off the sidewalk with free-play coupons, and lights so bright you can take photos at night without a flash. Las Vegas consumes more electricity per capita than any other community in the world. Any one of the major Strip or downtown casino hotels uses more electricity than the entire city of Santa Fe, New Mexico.

Lodging

Las Vegas offers good hotel room bargains in all price ranges. However, if you're arriving without reservations, you may quickly discover that the city is booked to near-capacity on weekends and fills up almost every weekday evening. The best emergency room-search strategy is to drive directly to **Circus Circus**, park in the huge free lot behind the hotel, and work your way through the casino to the front desk, where, if they don't have a vacancy among their 2,800 rooms (priced around $42 on week-days), they guarantee to place you in another hotel within your budget.

The following price ranges are approximate, since room rates change constantly according to demand. Rates are always lower Sunday through Thursday.

Las Vegas' top traditional luxury hotel is **Caesars Palace**, 3750 Las Vegas Boulevard South, toll-free (800) 634-6661; rates for doubles are about $105 to $160. As opulent as Caesars Palace is the newest hotel on the Strip, the **Mirage**, 3400 Las Vegas Boulevard South. Room rates run $89 on weekdays, $159 on weekends. For reservations, call toll-free (800) 627-6667. A close competitor when it comes to elegance in casino hotels is **Bally's-Las Vegas**, formerly the MGM Grand Hotel, at 3645 Las Vegas Boulevard South, toll-free (800) 634-3434. Rooms at Bally's cost $79 to $150. Reservations at Bally's can also be made through Las Vegas Hotel Reservations, (800) 446-5708, which also books rooms for the **Flamingo Hilton** ($65 to $115), the **Riviera** ($59 to $95), the **Imperial Palace** ($45 to $100), and the **Hacienda Resort Hotel** ($36 to $86), all on the Strip, as well as the **Las Vegas Hilton** ($75 to $160) near the convention center and the **Union Plaza** (around $40) and **Lady Luck** ($39 to $69) hotels downtown. Other midrange casino hotels include the New Orleans-style **Four Queens**, 202 East Fremont Street (downtown), toll-free (800) 634-6045, $47 to $57; **Circus Circus**, 2880 Las Vegas Boulevard South, toll-free (800) 634-6833 from Arizona, California, Utah, or Idaho, (800) 634-3450 from other states, about $42; and the **Maxim Hotel**, 160 East Flamingo Road (close to Bally's and Caesars Palace), toll-free (800) 634-6987, $40 to $68. The lowest room prices on the Strip—$32 to $36—are at the **Motel Monaco**, 3073 Las Vegas Boulevard South, (702) 735-9222.

Las Vegas has no B&Bs or period restoration hotels. If the casino hotel scene is not for you, the region's best historic hotel is **Boulder Dam Hotel**, 1305 Arizona Street, Boulder City, (702) 293-1808, a reasonably priced

colonial-style 1930s hotel originally built for dignitaries
visiting Hoover Dam, recently renovated, with period
furnishings. Gambling is prohibited in Boulder City.

Camping

Circusland, the 420-site RV campground operated by
Circus Circus, behind the hotel, (702) 734-0410, same
toll-free numbers as the hotel, bills itself as "The World's
Finest RV Park." Well. . . the scenery may leave something to be desired, but it *is* within convenient walking
distance of the "World's Largest Curio Shop." Amenities
include a pool, Jacuzzi, children's playground, laundry
and 24-hour convenience store, and full hookups, $10
per night. An elevated tramway carries campers to the
hotel's casino.

Sightseeing Highlights: Casino Hotels

Some of the more famous Strip casino hotels, such as the
Desert Inn (where Howard Hughes's penthouse was
located) and the Sands (Ronald Reagan's favorite), are
traditional, comparatively dignified country club-style
resorts that feature golf, tennis, and swimming pools but
not much to invite sightseeing by nonguests. Other
casinos will go to any length to attract attention. Here are
the most unusual sights on and near the Strip, from north
to south:

▲ **Bob Stupak's Vegas World**—It's the one with the
big silver rocket in front. See the building-size mural of
the moon and the earth, and don't miss the fiber-optic
model of the solar system on the lobby ceiling or the
Apollo Skylab replica.

▲▲ **Circus Circus**—Imagine the bizarre burst of crea-
tive thought that inspired the construction of this pink
and white striped building in the shape of a circus tent,
paid for by computers that play poker (and win). Circus
Circus was the first casino designed with families in
mind. The mezzanine has a midway of carnival games
(prizes are offered, but no gambling) and the latest in
video games, as well as a merry-go-round bar overlook-

ing the casino. The midway is a good place from which to watch circus acts, which are performed above the casino on the hour from 11:00 a.m. to midnight.

▲ **Las Vegas Hilton**—Easy to spot, several blocks off the Strip and just north of the convention center, the central attraction here is Benihana Village, a Japanese restaurant and lounge complex patterned after a temple courtyard. Light shows and fountains simulate fireworks and thunderstorms. The Imperial Room, the Hilton's French restaurant, displays replicas of the British crown jewels.

▲ **The Landmark**—Midway between the Hilton and the Strip on Convention Center Drive, this instantly recognizable Space Needle-style tower, which Howard Hughes built, affords the best nighttime view of Las Vegas' lights from the lounge, restaurants, and nightclub on the top floors.

▲ **Imperial Palace**—This pagoda-shaped hotel houses a fifth-floor showroom with one of the finest vintage automobile collections anywhere, 200 cars including Hitler's Mercedes and Al Capone's Cadillac. The car museum is open daily from 9:00 a.m. to 11:30 p.m. Admission to the museum is $3.75 for adults, $2 for children ages 5 to 12 and seniors over 65.

▲▲▲ **Mirage**—This new luxury casino hotel, under the same ownership as the Golden Nugget downtown, is located just north of Caesars Palace on the same side of the Strip. You can't miss the "volcano" out front, which erupts nightly and has a man-made waterfall. Inside, you'll find a European shopping area and a 60-foot atrium containing a rain forest and more waterfalls. The hotel's most unique attraction is a habitat for rare, live white tigers owned by magicians Siegfried and Roy.

▲▲▲ **Caesars Palace**—For sheer unabashed spectacle, Caesars Palace is unrivaled. If you visit only one Strip casino, make it this one. Starting from the corner of Flamingo and the Strip, ride the moving sidewalk past fountains, cypress trees, and replicas of ancient statues, as the voice of Caesar urges you on. From the front entrance, go around to the right of the main casino to see

Cleopatra's Barge (a full-size replica that serves as a float-ing dance floor and lounge) and bigger-than-life replicas of two Michelangelo statues. Take a look at the Olympiad Race and Sports Book, with its 19-foot-by-26-foot TV screen plus 19 other TV screens, each showing live cover-age of a different sporting event. Farther in the same direction is the Omnimax Theater—movie thrills on a wraparound projection dome. Call 731-7900 for current show information. Around on the west side of the hotel, the pool area, the Garden of the Gods, is a replica of the baths of Pompeii. Peek in if you can't sneak in. Climb the grand staircase for a glimpse into the private rooms where baccarat is played for high stakes. Finally, don't miss the Brahma Shrine, imported from Thailand, on the north lawn. The hotel provides incense and flowers for wor-shipers. If this shrine seems strangely out of place amid all the macho neo-Romanism, take a look around and see how many Asian tourists visit Las Vegas. Caesars Palace is building a new 150-store retail complex to be known as the Forum. When it is completed in 1990, it promises to be the most expensive shopping district in Las Vegas; it will also have an outdoor "Roman Village Bazaar."

▲▲ **Bally's-Las Vegas**—Originally built by MGM motion picture studios as a lavish tribute to an earlier era of big-screen Hollywood opulence, this huge crystal-and-marble grand hotel burned down in 1980 and was rebuilt with even more elegance; then it was sold to Bally's, the corporation that makes slot machines, pinball machines, and video games. The casino is still the largest in town, and the movie house with its romantic loveseats still shows classic films (three showings nightly plus two matinees each weekend day, $3.50 for adults, $2.75 for children under 12, $2 for senior citizens).

▲ **The Dunes**—Amid Arabic ambience, look for the Xanadunes video game area—all the newest and flashiest—by the black-glass domed casino with its neon palm trees. The Dunes, like the Aladdin and several other Las Vegas hotels, was purchased recently by Japanese investors.

Other Sightseeing Highlights

▲ **Museum of Natural History**—On the University of Nevada-Las Vegas campus, off Tropicana midway between Paradise Road and Maryland Parkway, the museum features desert exhibits that range from Native American arts and crafts to dinosaur fossils to live rattlesnakes behind glass. Open daily 9:00 a.m. to 9:00 p.m.; admission is $5.50 for adults, $2.50 for children under age 12.

▲ **Liberace Museum**—This monument to conspicuous consumption is pretty strange even for Las Vegas. See the late Lee Liberace's piano collection, limousines, furs, and 115,000-karat rhinestone at 1775 East Tropicana, between Maryland Parkway and Eastern Avenue, east of the Strip. The museum is open Monday through Saturday from 10:00 a.m. to 5:00 p.m. and Sundays from 1:00 to 5:00 p.m. Admission is $6.50 for adults, $4.50 for those over age 60, $3.50 for students, and $2 for children age 6 to 12.

▲ **Nevada State Museum and Historical Society**—Local history as well as plant, animal, and Indian exhibits are housed in this modern adobe-style building at 700 Twin Lakes Drive, adjoining Lorenzi Park. Take Sahara Avenue west from the Strip to Valley View Road, turn north (right) and continue to Bonanza Road, just past the Las Vegas Expressway. Turn right on Bonanza and you're there. The museum is open Monday and Tuesday from 11:30 a.m. to 4:30 p.m. and Wednesday through Sunday from 8:30 a.m. to 4:30 p.m. Admission is $1 for adults, free for people under age 18.

▲ **Las Vegas Art Museum**—Across the park from the state museum, the art museum (built of railroad ties) is a relic from Twin Lakes Resort, which occupied the present-day city park back in the 1920s and 1930s. The museum, exhibiting works by local artists, may help dispel the impression that Las Vegas is a cultural wasteland. Open Tuesday through Saturday from 10:00 a.m. to 4:00 p.m., Sundays from 12:00 noon to 4:00 p.m., closed Mondays; free admission.

▲ **Ripley's Believe It or Not! Museum**—Downtown at the Four Queens Hotel, this hall of sensationalism, along with several other Ripley's museums around the United States, has been attracting tourists for forty years. Today it has a certain quaintness. Believe it or not, this is the only place in the Southwest where you can see a real shrunken head. Open Sunday through Thursday from 10:00 a.m. to 12:00 midnight, Friday and Saturday from 9:00 a.m. to 1:00 a.m. Admission is $4.95 for adults, $3.95 for those over 50, and $2.50 for children ages 6 to 12.

▲ **Old Mormon Fort**—This restored fort at Washington and Las Vegas Boulevard was the first settlement in the Las Vegas area, built in 1855 as a way station for travelers between Salt Lake City and Los Angeles. Open Saturday and Monday 8:00 a.m. to 2:00 p.m. and Sunday 12:00 noon to 3:00 p.m. during the summer months, Monday and Saturday 10:00 a.m. to 4:00 p.m. and Sunday 1:00 to 4:00 p.m. the rest of the year; closed Tuesday through Friday. Admission is $1 for adults, $0.50 for children under 12.

Food

The most self-indulgent dining in Las Vegas, if you can get reservations, is the lavish **Bacchanal** at Caesars Palace, complete with scantily clad "wine goddesses." The cost is about $60 per person. Seatings are Tuesday through Sunday at 6:00 to 6:30 p.m. and 9:00 to 9:30 p.m., closed Mondays. Reservations are required—call 731-7110 or make them at the hotel desk. Also in Caeser's Palace, **Primavera** serves pricey Italian food overlooking the hotel's Garden of the Gods swimming pool.

Other interesting dining possibilities in the casino hotels include **Tracy's** in Bally's (Continental, open Friday through Tuesday 5:00 to 11:00 p.m.); the **Ming Terrace** in the Imperial Palace (Chinese, open 12:00 noon to 12:00 midnight); **The Steak House** in Circus Circus (American, 5:00 p.m. to 12:00 midnight); and **Benihana Village** in the Las Vegas Hilton (Japanese, 6:00 to 11:00 p.m.). All casino hotels also have 24-hour coffee shops, typically with super-efficient waitresses and almost instant service. Many casinos offer incredibly cheap breakfasts, $0.69 to $1.99, in efforts to attract the last of the up-all-night crowd during the morning hours when business is slow. But the best food bargain in town—breakfast, lunch, or dinner—is the all-you-can-eat buffets served at many casino hotels. They run from $4 to $8, with champagne often served at the more expensive ones, and because of growing competition they vie in true Las Vegas style for the "most sumptuous spread" title. Look for buffets at Caesars Palace, the Mirage, Bally's, the Imperial Palace, Circus Circus, the Flamingo Hilton, or any of several other Strip casinos. They are often advertised on the hotels' marquees. Outside of the hotels, local favorite Las Vegas restaurants include **Battista's Hole in the Wall**, a moderately priced Italian restaurant known as a show business hangout, behind Bally's at 4041 Audrie Street, open nightly 5:00 to 11:00 p.m., reservations essential—call 732-1424; the **Starboard Tack**, serving steaks and seafood in the most nautical ambience to be found in the whole Mojave Desert at 2601 Atlantic Avenue (off Sahara one block east of Eastern), 457-8794, open Monday through Friday from 11:30 a.m. to 6:00 a.m. and Friday and Saturday from 5:00 p.m. to 6:00 a.m.; and **Flakey Jake's**, which offers the biggest build-it-yourself hamburgers in town at 2870 S. Maryland Parkway (east of the Strip between Desert Inn Road and E. Sahara Avenue), open 11:00 a.m. to 10:00 p.m. daily.

Ethel M Chocolates Factory at 2 Cactus Garden Drive, Henderson (take Tropicana Boulevard east and watch for signs; there is also a retail outlet downtown), 452-7805, makes delicious liqueur-filled chocolates that are only sold in Nevada. Epicures everywhere lust for them. The candy factory was started by the late Ethel Mars, who invented Mars Bars and M&Ms, then retired here to create masterpieces. Take the free tour, try a few samples, and soon you'll have to figure out what to do with boxes of chocolates in 100-degree heat. Hint: take them back to your air-conditioned hotel room. Then eat them.

Shows and Nightlife

In addition to free lounge acts (from rising stars to nearly laughable also-ran crooners) just off the casino floor, all major casino hotels have showrooms where performances are generally priced from $20 to $50 (including dinner at the early show around 8:00 p.m. or drinks at the midnight show). Las Vegas hotels pay performers higher than any other nightclubs in the nation, and big names and flawless big-budget productions are everywhere up and down the Strip. On any given night you'll face a choice of entertainers ranging from longtime Vegas favorites like Wayne Newton, Sammy Davis, Jr., Tony Bennett, Neil Diamond, and Englebert Humperdinck to famous "newcomers" like Dolly Parton, Eddie Murphy, the Neville Brothers, and Alabama. In addition to frequently changing big-name performers, many hotels stage permanent "extravaganzas" full of chorus lines, special effects, and elaborate sets and costumes. Among them are Bally's *Jubilee*, the Tropicana's *Folies Bergere*, the Stardust's *Lido de Paris*, and the Riviera's *An Evening at La Cage*. The best magic shows anywhere are in Las Vegas; don't pass up a chance to see David Copperfield or Siegfried and Roy if they're in town when you are.

Most shows change frequently. Schedules and reservations are available three to four months in advance from the Las Vegas Chamber of Commerce, 2301 East Sahara, (702)-457-5544. (Most travel agents around the nation can also provide Las Vegas show schedules.) On short notice, it is easiest to get tickets for the show at the hotel where you are staying. Entertainment schedules are published in the Thursday *Las Vegas Sun* and Friday *Las Vegas Review-Journal* newspapers.

Most cultural events (sponsored by the Las Vegas Arts Alliance) and rock concerts are held at the University of Nevada-Las Vegas. Performance information is available 24 hours a day by calling 739-3131.

A Word about Gambling

Many casinos offer "fun books," coupons you get from the cashier by showing an out-of-state driver's license along with a flyer distributed at tourist information booths, service stations, and restaurants outside Clark County. The books lure you with offers of freebies ranging from breakfast to candy and cocktails, discounts on rooms, meals, and shows, and free play on certain slot machines. Some of these special free-play machines have the odds rigged in your favor—to let you win. Free money? Don't bet on it. The house knows that once you start gambling, it doesn't matter how much of their money you win. They've got plenty more. You'll keep playing until you lose your money. ("Not me," everybody says until they try it.) That phenomenon of human nature keeps Las Vegas residents employed and pays for all the ostentation and electricity.

Besides the loudest wallpaper on earth (designed by experts to drive you out of the room and down to the casino), hotel guest rooms feature "how to gamble" programming on closed-circuit TV. For visitors who are ready to move up from slot machines to higher-stakes games of chance, several casinos offer free gambling classes. The Imperial Palace has a fourth-floor gambling school where you can practice with fake chips—roulette and blackjack lessons at 9:00 a.m. and 1:00 p.m., craps at 11:00 a.m. and 3:00 p.m. Other hotels such as the Riviera, the Tropicana, and both Hiltons give gambling instruction in special areas of the casino. The Las Vegas Hilton will show you how baccarat works, and the Frontier teaches poker. Advance registration is not necessary, and the lessons are free (in a manner of speaking).

Gaming revenues in Las Vegas exceed $2 billion per year. That's nearly $4,000 a year for each man, woman, and child in the city. Visitors' gambling losses average $154.

LAS VEGAS TO FLAGSTAFF

Cross the Colorado River at either Hoover Dam or Laughlin/Bullhead City and drive to Flagstaff via a forgotten section of old Route 66. Or sleep late, cross Hoover Dam into Arizona, and take the interstate direct to Flagstaff.

Suggested Schedule

9:00 a.m.	Breakfast.
10:00 a.m.	Drive to Laughlin.
11:30 a.m.	Ferry across the Colorado River to Bullhead City.
12:00 noon	Lunch, then drive to Flagstaff.
4:00 p.m.	Arrive in Flagstaff. Check into accommodations or drive and find a campsite near Sunset Crater.

Travel Route: Las Vegas to Flagstaff: Direct (249 miles) or Scenic (290 miles)

Depending on how much fun you had last night, you may not feel like getting up early. The first two hours of today's drive will be through hot, hilly desert, a good argument for getting an early start. However, if you cross the desert under the midday sun, reaching shady pine forests this afternoon will be all the more pleasurable.

Direct Route: To drive directly from Las Vegas to Flagstaff, go east to the Boulder Highway (US 93; from the Strip, Desert Inn Road or Tropicana Road will take you there) and south through Boulder City to Hoover Dam. Continue on US 93—straight, two-lane, up and down barren hills—to Kingman, where you'll meet I-40 (the distance from Las Vegas is 102 miles).

Kingman is the world's leading producer of jewelry-grade turquoise. The **Mohave Museum of History and Arts**, a quarter-mile east of the Beale Street exit from I-40, features displays of regional history from prehistoric times to the present, a miniature Mohave Indian village

Las Vegas to Kingman

diorama, the Colbaugh Collection of carved turquoise, and a whole room memorializing Kingman's most famous native son, the late actor Andy Devine ("Hey, Wild Bill, wait for me!"). From Kingman, go eastbound, 147 more fast miles to Flagstaff.

Scenic Route: To take the alternate route from Las Vegas to Kingman, 123 miles (as compared to 102), leave the Boulder Highway on US 95, where the sign says "Searchlight/Needles," just before Boulder City. Go 54 miles south on this highway, then turn left (east) on NV 163. It's 21 miles to Davis Dam, which contains Lake Mojave (the next Colorado River reservoir south of Lake Mead). The highway crosses the dam into Arizona, where it becomes AZ 68; but instead, take a short (3-mile) side trip south to **Laughlin**, Nevada's southernmost town.

Laughlin consists entirely of casinos, while resort accommodations are across the river in the larger town of **Bullhead City**, Arizona. Passenger ferries were the only way
to cross from the hotels on the Arizona side to the gaming
tables on the Nevada side until recently. Now there is an
automobile bridge, but the ferry still runs, and the mini-
cruise provides a pleasant driving break. From Bullhead
City, drive 3 miles back north to AZ 68 and, from there,
east 29 more miles to Kingman.

(For adventurous drivers in the spring and fall months,
a more challenging route to Kingman exits just south of
Bullhead City and Bullhead County Park to take you over
the crest of the Sacramento Mountains, through the picturesque former ghost town of **Oatman**, where cowboy
actors now stage "shootouts" on weekends, and the ruins
of still-abandoned Goldroad. The route, 40 miles from
Bullhead City to Kingman, isn't much longer than taking
the main highway, but it's much slower. About 8 miles are
unpaved.)

The alternate route from Kingman to Flagstaff (167
miles, as compared to 147 via the interstate) follows AZ 66
from I-40 exit 53, the easternmost Kingman exit, to
return to the interstate at Seligman. This little-used two-
lane highway was formerly part of the first paved highway across the Southwest to southern California. Route
66 captured the imagination of America's post-World War
II generation and was immortalized by musicians from
Glen Miller to the Rolling Stones, as well as by a popular
1960s TV series. Today, most of old Route 66 has become

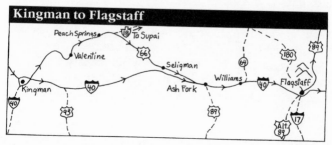

Kingman to Flagstaff

I-40. This remote 93-mile stretch was bypassed. Drive it and feel what the Southwest's main highway was like 40 years ago.

The only sightseeing attraction (or sign of recent habitation) along old Route 66 is **Grand Canyon Caverns**, a large limestone cave 200 feet underground, reached by elevator. The cost of the 45-minute tour is $5.75 for adults, $3.75 for children ages 6 to 14. The adjacent Caverns Inn has barbecue cookouts, camping, a motel, a restaurant, a cocktail lounge, gift shops, a minimarket, a gas station, and an airstrip. As at many tourist caves, there's a huge dinosaur statue by the entrance. About 2 miles before the caverns is the turnoff to Supai (see Itinerary Option).

Route 66 returns to the interstate at Seligman, 74 miles from Flagstaff. The drive from Ash Fork to Flagstaff is the most scenic segment of I-40 west of Arkansas.

Camping

To reach Coconino National Forest's **Bonito Campground**, across from the visitors center at the south boundary of Sunset Crater, take the third Flagstaff exit (#201) and turn north on US 89. Go 10 miles to the turnoff for Sunset Crater National Monument. Bonito Campground is on your left at the monument boundary, across the road from the Sunset Crater visitors center.

The campground is large, popular, and remarkably spacious. It often fills by 6:00 p.m., so stake out your campsite early, before taking the Sunset Crater-Wupatki drive. Volunteers from the National Monument present campfire talks nightly during the summer months. From the upper end of the campground, you can easily walk a mile or more over the cinder fields along the edge of the jagged lava flow, finding several good views of the lava and of O'Leary Crater. An unpaved road starts just east of the campground and goes 5 miles to the summit of the volcano.

Lodging

The **Hotel Weatherford**, (602) 774-2731, at the corner
of N. Leroux Street and Aspen Avenue, a block north of
the railroad station in downtown Flagstaff, was the most
elegant hotel in town when it opened in 1897. Now a
youth hostel, the Weatherford also offers several rather
spartan private hotel rooms for under $25 double. For the
young at heart, the absence of guest room decor is more
than compensated for by the lively social scene. An international crowd of mostly young travelers congregates in
the second-floor lobby nightly, while Charly's Pub on
the ground floor is popular among local college students.
The adjoining restaurant serves homemade soups,
breads, desserts, and good dinners.

Another historic downtown hotel, the **Monte Vista** at
100 N. San Francisco St., (602) 774-6971, offers guest
rooms remodeled in 1927 decor. Rates range from $38 to
$74 double. **Dierker House**, at 423 W. Cherry, (602)
774-3249, offers bed and breakfast for two at about $40.

The 3-mile I-40 business loop north of downtown is
lined with motels. The "brand-name" chain motels range
from moderate (around $40 double at the **Imperial 400**
and **Regal 8**) to expensive (around $75 double at the
Best Western Little America and **Holiday Inn**). A
plethora of independent "ma-and-pa" motels offer much
lower rates, typically $25 to $35 double, on marquees
signs out front. Cruise the motel strip and pick the place
that appeals to you. "No vacancy" problems are unlikely
as long as you arrive in Flagstaff by 6:00 p.m.

Food

Flagstaff's student population supports a wide variety of
reasonably priced, informal restaurants in the downtown
area. For Mexican food, try **El Charro**, 409 S. San Francisco, or the **Burrito Palace** at 10 N. San Francisco.
Good Chinese food is served at the **Hong Kong Cafe**, 6
E. Santa Fe Avenue, and the **Grand Canyon Cafe**, 110 E.
Santa Fe. For good American food, eat at **Charly's** in the

Hotel Weatherford. For fine Continental dining, the intimate place to go in Flagstaff is the **Cottage Place**, a small house two blocks south of downtown at 126 W. Cottage Avenue, open Tuesday through Sunday 5:00 to 9:30 p.m., closed Mondays.

The series of shopping centers along Milton Road (US 89A), which runs south from downtown between the railroad tracks and the interstate, offers a selection of supermarkets. For more specialized food shopping, visit **Winnie's Natural Foods**, downtown at the corner of Santa Fe Avenue and San Francisco Street.

Itinerary Option

Shortly before Grand Canyon Caverns on old Route 66 is a turnoff marked "Supai." What the sign doesn't mention is that the isolated Indian village of **Supai** is down in Havasu Canyon, a branch of the Grand Canyon. On the Supai road, the pavement ends 62 miles from the turnoff; 11 miles later, at Hualapai Hilltop, the road ends, and it's another 8 miles by foot trail, descending 2,000 feet, to Supai. The trail continues to Havasu Falls and the Colorado River. Consider this trek if you're a serious hiker with plenty of extra time (at least two days) and a desire to hike into the Grand Canyon. Backpacker camping is allowed only in two tribal campgrounds along Havasu Creek ($7). Supai has a café, a food store, and a post office as well as a lodge ($35 double). You must pay the tribe an $8 entrance fee upon arrival in Supai. Reservations are essential, even for camping. Contact Havasupai Tourist Enterprise, Supai, AZ 86435, (602) 448-2121.

FLAGSTAFF

Flagstaff, just 2½ highway hours from the big city of Phoenix and 1½ from Grand Canyon Village on the South Rim, is northern Arizona's tourist hub. Don't bother moving your campsite or changing motel rooms. Within a few minutes' drive from the city are enough unusual and enjoyable attractions to fill your whole day and then some.

Suggested Schedule

9:00 a.m.	Breakfast.
10:00 a.m.	See Walnut Canyon National Monument.
12:00 noon	Lunch in downtown Flagstaff.
1:15 p.m.	Lowell Observatory (1:30 tour).
2:30 p.m.	Drive down Oak Creek Canyon to Sedona.
Later	Return to Flagstaff. Spend the night at the same lodging or campground as last night.

Flagstaff

The largest city on I-40 west of Albuquerque, Flagstaff (pop. 40,000) was founded in 1881 as a railroad town (the railroad actually reached Flagstaff in 1882). The University of Northern Arizona strikes a cultural counterpoint to Flagstaff's tourist-and-truck-stop aspect.

Historic downtown Flagstaff is at the extreme west end of town. Don't be put off by the trackside heavy industry you see from the interstate or the motel strip business route. Downtown Flagstaff, between Humphreys and Agassiz streets due north of the railroad station on Santa Fe Avenue, is a low-key, low-priced, and generally underrated historic district. Stroll it.

Sightseeing Highlights

▲▲ **Walnut Canyon National Monument**—Just 3 miles off the interstate from exit 204 east of town, Walnut

Canyon offers a one-hour walk on a paved trail around an "island" above the canyon to see about a hundred small 800-year-old cliff dwellings of the Sinagua Indians. Look-but-don't-touch views of the pristine wooded canyon floor enhance the experience. Open 7:00 a.m. to 7:00 p.m. Memorial Day to Labor Day, 8:00 a.m. to 5:00 p.m. the rest of the year. Admission is $3 per vehicle.

▲▲ **Lowell Observatory**—Follow the winding road from the west end of Santa Fe Avenue up to this hilltop observatory, founded by wealthy Boston businessman-turned-astronomer Percival Lowell in 1894, just 13 years after Flagstaff became a town. Lowell is best remembered for "discovering" the (nonexistent) canals of Mars and hypothesizing an ancient Martian civilization. One may wonder whether Indian ruins around Flagstaff helped guide his vivid imagination. Based on Lowell's theoretical predictions of a ninth planet, Dr. Clyde Tombaugh discovered Pluto from this observatory in 1930. The "red shift" of galaxies, upon which the theory of the expanding universe is based, was also discovered here. Lowell's original telescope in its old wooden observatory tower looks like an antique left over from a Victorian science fiction novel, ideal for Martian-watching. The visitors center is open June through August only, Tuesday through Saturday, 10:00 a.m. to 4:30 p.m. Tours start at 10:00 a.m. and 1:30 p.m. June through September, 1:30 p.m. only the rest of the year. You can look through the telescope between 8:00 and 10:00 p.m. on any Friday night June through August or the first night of any other month. Suggested donations are $1 per person or $3 per family. For prerecorded information, call 774-2096.

▲ **Museum of Northern Arizona**—This museum, located 3 miles north of downtown Flagstaff on US 180, houses one of the most comprehensive archaeology, ethnology, geology, biology, and fine arts collections in the Southwest. In July, the annual Hopi and Navajo Craftsman Exhibitions draw visitors and collectors from all over the United States. The museum is open daily from 9:00 a.m. to 5:00 p.m.

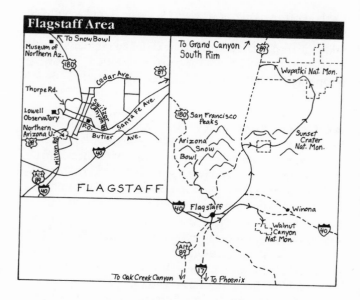

▲ **The Arboretum at Flagstaff**—Arizona flora native
to the alpine tundra, evergreen forest, and high desert are
exhibited here. Guided tours are Monday through Friday,
starting regularly from 10:00 a.m. to 3:00 p.m. Follow old
Route 66 from South Milton near downtown, turning left
on unpaved Woody Mountain Road, a total distance of
about 4 miles.

▲ **Fairfield Snow Bowl**—In the San Francisco Peaks,
this is the state's highest and best winter downhill ski area
and a popular summer hiking trailhead. In the summer
months, the chair lift carries sightseers to the summit of
Mt. Humphries (11,500 ft.) for a spectacular view of Flagstaff, Sunset Crater/Wupatki, the surrounding forest and
volcano fields, and the Grand Canyon in the distance. Follow US 180 for 7 miles north from Flagstaff, then turn
right and go another 7 miles on an unpaved road. The lift
operates from 10:00 a.m. until 4:00 p.m. in the summer
months, weekends only in September and October. Tickets cost $7 for adults and $3.50 for children ages 6 to 12.

▲▲ **Oak Creek Canyon and Sedona**—From downtown Flagstaff, go west on Santa Fe Avenue, staying on the same street as it veers south to become Milton Road, which is lined with shopping centers. Get in the right-hand lane. Just before Milton crosses under the interstate, take the fork to the right, following signs to US 89A, Oak Creek Canyon, and Sedona.

The 27-mile drive from Flagstaff to Sedona through Oak Creek Canyon plunges from ponderosa forest to red rock desert. Scattered with summer cabins and resorts, the canyon road is a well-known and popular scenic drive. In July and August as well as early October (autumn colors), don't expect to find a parking place, let alone a campsite, in any of the canyon's five national forest camp-grounds. Slide Rock, midway down the canyon on your right, was traditionally the local "beach" for University of Northern Arizona students. It has recently become an Arizona state park, and new regulations have restricted the once wet and wild scene.

Sedona, at the lower end of the canyon, is a booming resort town. Grown from a handful of residents to a year-round population of 12,000 in just twenty years, it has more millionaires per capita than any other municipality in the state. Scenically located at the base of the red rock cliffs that separate mountainous northern Arizona from the hot desert of southern Arizona, Sedona is considered by some to be a wonderful vacation spot. Judge for yourself.

Itinerary Option: Jerome

Jerome, 30 miles beyond Sedona, was the site of environ-mental plunder on a grand scale; paradoxically, it is one of the most interesting communities in central Arizona. Named after a cousin of Jenny Jerome (Winston Chur-chill's mother), the town had a population of 15,000 near the end of the nineteenth century, most of the residents living in tents. In 72 years, $800,000,000 worth of copper was dug from the mountainside, along with modest amounts of gold and silver. (Imagine 80 billion pennies. Stacked, they would make a column 63,000 miles tall; laid in a row, they would reach almost a million miles. You could pave every inch of the U.S. interstate highway system with pennies and have more than a million dollars left over.) Jerome was destroyed by fire three times in three years (1897-1899). One of the fires, a Prescott newspaper reported, wiped out the entire downtown area, consisting of 24 saloons, 14 Chinese restaurants, several casinos, and the red-light district. After the third fire, the town was rebuilt in brick. Jerome was abandoned in 1953, but the turn-of-the-century buildings survived.

Jerome is a National Historic District. Since the 1960s it has been repopulated, mainly by artists and craftspeople, to a present population of 450. You can visit the Gold King Mine and Museum, the Jerome Historical Society Mine Museum, and/or the Jerome State Historic Park Museum and Douglas Mansion for further historical insights, but the town's real charm is to be found along Main Street, with its folksy array of art galleries, hippie eateries, and rock shops.

To get there, drive 19 miles beyond Sedona on US 89A to Bridgeport. Turn right (north) on AZ 279 and drive 11 more miles, through the Verde Valley agricultural towns of Cottonwood and Clarkdale, then up the mountainside to Jerome.

THE GRAND CANYON: SOUTH RIM

It's still the same canyon you saw on Day 14. But the
South Rim is different. For one thing, there's a big new
McDonald's near the main park gates (you'll use a different entrance). En route, tour Sunset Crater and Wupatki
national monuments to see some of the Southwest's most
striking volcanic landscapes.

Suggested Schedule

8:00 a.m.	Get an early start. Campgrounds and lodg-ing accommodations at Grand Canyon Village fill up fast.
8:30 a.m.	Visit Sunset Crater.
9:30 a.m.	Take the scenic drive through Sunset Cra-ter and Wupatki national monuments.
12:00 noon	Drive to the Grand Canyon.
1:30 p.m.	Arrive at Grand Canyon Village. Check into the campground or lodging, then eat a late lunch.
3:00 p.m.	Ride the shuttle bus along West Rim Drive.
4:30 p.m.	Visit the visitors center, then walk over to the corral to watch the mule trip return up Bright Angel Trail.
Evening	Another Grand Canyon sunset.

Travel Route: Flagstaff to Grand Canyon South Rim (121 miles)

From I-40 on the eastern edge of Flagstaff, turn north on
US 89. Go 10 miles to the turnoff for Sunset Crater
National Monument. From Sunset Crater, a 36-mile road
takes you north to the Wupatki visitors center and then
through Wupatki National Monument. Rejoining US 86,
turn right and go north for about 20 more miles to the
intersection with AZ 64. Turn west, and another 55 miles
will bring you to Grand Canyon Village.

The entrance fee to the Grand Canyon is $5 per vehi-
cle. Your fee receipt from the North Rim, if paid within
the last 7 days, will get you into the South Rim as well.

Sightseeing Highlights
▲▲ **Sunset Crater National Monument**—Thousand-foot-tall Sunset Crater is the most impressive of about a dozen volcano cones that dot the forest north of Flagstaff and west of San Francisco Peaks. These volcanoes are remarkable because they are so new. Sunset Crater began erupting in the winter of A.D. 1064-65 and continued to spew cinders for almost two centuries until A.D. 1250, just an eyeblink ago in geological time. Today, scientists and tourists alike watch in suspense for rare, foreboding rumbles on the seismograph in the visitors center.

Sunset Crater is no longer very accessible to hikers. The volcano cone itself is closed to hiking (increased tourist traffic made too many unsightly footprints across the cinders); an ice cave, which was the second-best attraction, collapsed a few years ago. Today, only a short nature trail is open for walking. From the visitors center, rangers guide an assortment of other hikes as well as jeep trips up nearby O'Leary Crater outside the monument. Combined admission to Sunset Crater and Wupatki national monuments is $3 per vehicle.

▲▲ **Wupatki National Monument**—Farming Indians who lived in pithouses here in the eleventh century abandoned the area when Sunset Crater began to erupt. When the fireworks stopped, the porous volcanic ash retained water for better farming. Indians from several cultures—Kayenta Anasazi, Sinagua, Hohokam, and Cohonina—resettled the area. The assortment of architecture and artifacts found within just a few miles is an archaeologist's field day.

▲▲▲ **Grand Canyon National Park: South Rim**—This is one of the most visited places in the national park system. Coming from Sunset Crater and Wupatki, you will enter the park through the less-used gates at the east end of East Rim Drive. On the way to Grand Canyon Village, you will see a replica **Hopi watchtower** and several well-marked points with spectacular views. Take time to stop at the **Tusayan ruin and museum** a few miles past the watchtower to learn about the Grand Canyon's

Anasazi past, as well as the **Yavapai Museum**, just before you reach the village, for geology and natural history exhibits. Both are free, open daily from 8:00 a.m. to 6:00 p.m. in the summer months and 9:00 a.m. to 5:00 p.m. the rest of the year. The main visitors center, just past the Yavapai Museum, is open from 8:00 a.m. to 7:00 p.m. during the summer months, until 5:00 p.m. the rest of the year.

Grand Canyon Village is big, congested with visitors, and crammed with concessionaires; the rest of the canyon rim is untouched by development. The **West Rim Drive** is closed to private vehicles during the summer months but accessible by free park service shuttle buses. The easy, paved **South Rim Nature Trail** runs 3½ miles along the rim between the Yavapai Museum, the hotel area, and the Powell Memorial on West Rim Drive.

The South Rim is most famous for its muleback trips down Bright Angel Trail. The trips are as popular as ever—so popular, in fact, that they are often booked up as much as a year in advance. To make reservations, contact Reservations Department, Grand Canyon National Park Lodge, P.O. Box 699, Grand Canyon, AZ 86023, (602) 638-2401. The cost is $64 per person, including lunch, for the one-day trip midway down the canyon, or $206 per person for an overnight trip to Phantom Ranch down on the river. Those who didn't plan that far ahead can check with the lodge to see if cancellations have created space on the next day's mule trip. You can walk over to the corral and watch the mule trips leave each morning around 9:00 to 9:30 and return around 4:30 or 5:00. You can also hike a portion of the **Bright Angel Trail** yourself. Take water. If you hike down this trail in the morning, you may face hot temperatures on the strenuous climb back up.

Just in case seeing the real thing isn't enough, an IMAX (semidome wraparound screen) theater in Tusayan near the main entrance gate, 7 miles south of Grand Canyon Village, shows a half-hour film that includes rafting and flying footage. Not to be outdone, the Galaxy 4 theaters just up the road show four different Grand Canyon movies in separate viewing areas. Admission to either place is $5, the same as the entrance fee to the real Grand Canyon.

Camping

To stay in the campground at Grand Canyon village, you must make reservations (at least a month in advance) by mail through TICKETRON Reservation Office, 401 Hackensack Avenue, Hackensack, NJ 07601, or by calling (602) 340-9033 or (213) 410-1720 and prepaying your camping fee with your Visa or MasterCard. Fees start at $10. There are private campgrounds outside the main gate, 7 miles south of Grand Canyon Village.

Lodging

The original hotel built on the rim of the Grand Canyon by Fred Harvey in 1905, **El Tovar** is still the most elegant of the several hotels in Grand Canyon Village. Room rates are from $90 to $130. Also on the rim are **Kachina Lodge** ($85 to $90), **Yavapai Lodge** ($69 to $75), **Maswik Lodge** ($57 to $85), and **Bright Angel Lodge and Cabins** ($35 to $95). They are all under the same management, and prices reflect the quality of the accommodations, from turn-of-the-century luxury to motel ordinary to log cabin rustic. Check-in time at all of the Grand Canyon Village lodges is 3:30. Reservations should be made far in advance by calling Grand Canyon National Park Lodges at (602) 638-2401.

   If you arrive without reservations and find no vacancies within the park, there is a cluster of large resort motels just outside the south entrance. Prices are pretty much the same as at the Grand Canyon Village lodges, and the view isn't as nice.

Food

Grand Canyon Village has restaurant concessionaires in all price ranges. The main dining room at **El Tovar** serves

Continental cuisine nightly from 5:00 to 10:00 p.m. as well as breakfast (6:30 to 11:00 a.m.) and luncheon (11:30 a.m. to 2:00 p.m.). There is also a steak house, a hamburger restaurant, a snack bar, and a campers' grocery store.

THE HOPI MESAS

From the well-developed industrial tourism of the Grand Canyon South Rim, travel this afternoon to one of the earth's loneliest corners—the traditional mesa-top villages of the Hopi, who have lived there since the peak of the Anasazi civilizations at Chaco and Mesa Verde.

Suggested Schedule

9:00 a.m.	Breakfast at El Tovar dining room and a leisurely morning gazing at the Grand Canyon.
12:00 noon	After lunch, leave the park and drive to Tuba City on the Navajo Reservation.
2:00 p.m.	At Tuba City, turn off toward the Hopi mesas.
4:00 p.m.	Visit Hopi Cultural Center. Check into your motel room or arrange to camp. Eat dinner at the cultural center.
6:00 p.m.	Stroll the mesa. Listen to the silence.

Travel Route: Grand Canyon Village to Second Mesa (177 miles)

Leave the Grand Canyon the same way you came in, along East Rim Drive and through the east entrance gate. Retrace yesterday's route to the intersection with US 89, a distance of 55 miles. Turn north on US 89 and go 16 miles, then turn east on US 160. Ten miles will bring you to Tuba City. Turn south there on AZ 264. A 57-mile drive will bring you to Oraibi, westernmost of the Hopi mesa villages, on Third Mesa. Continue on the same roller-coaster highway to the Hopi Cultural Center on Second Mesa.

The Hopi

When other Anasazi groups abandoned their desert pueblos and moved to the Rio Grande Valley, the Hopi stayed in their mesa-top villages. The mesa contains an underground aquifer that has sustained the Hopi people's small, sandy fields—separate patches for red, white, blue, and yellow corn, all planted 18 inches deep—for a thousand years. The most remote of the Pueblo people, they were less influenced by missionaries than other ancient communities like Ácoma were. As recently as the end of World War II, when the first school was built at Keams Canyon, no Hopi spoke English. About that time, curious scientists, writers, artists, photographers, and sightseers began visiting the Hopi mesas, sometimes disrupting kachina and snake dances until finally outsiders were banned from most Hopi ceremonies.

Hopi villagers have a way of making sightseers feel invisible. This is not hostility; it's just a helpful tool for maintaining an eleventh-century agrarian culture in the 1990s. You can drive to most of the villages and wander freely. If you're interested in buying pottery, women who make and sell it may let you look inside their studios. All photography and sketching is strictly prohibited.

On Third Mesa, **Old Oraibi** has still-occupied homes that date back to about A.D. 1125, making it the oldest continuously inhabited community in the United States. The village is often off-limits to the public, but at other unpredictable times, visitors are admitted for a small fee.

On Second Mesa, at the **Hopi Cultural Center,** you'll find excellent exhibits on Hopi customs and crafts. The center is open daily from 9:00 a.m. to 5:00 p.m. MST (see About Time, below). The fixed-price Hopi arts and crafts shops nearby are a good place to buy quality work. **Shungopavi**, the tribal religious center, and the smaller Second Mesa villages **Shipaulovi** and **Mishongnovi**, were all built around A.D. 1700 by people who had formerly lived below the mesa. The ruins of a previous village, **Maseeba**, can be seen from an overlook at Shungopavi.

Polacca is a twentieth-century village. **Walpi**, on the tip of First Mesa, dates back to about A.D. 1400. Two

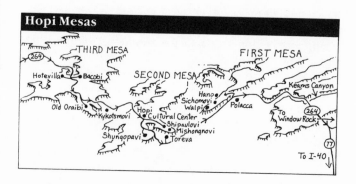

Hopi Mesas

eighteenth-century villages, **Sichomovi** and **Hano**—the latter formed by immigrant Pueblo people who fled from New Mexico after the Pueblo Revolt of 1680—are suburbs of Walpi.

Camping

Camp on the Hopi Reservation at the free **Second Mesa Campground and Trailer Park** next to the Cultural Center. You won't find water or hookups, but you can use the rest rooms and other services at the center. Other campgrounds are located below the mesas at **Keams Canyon** and at **Kykotsmovi**, a mile east of New Oraibi.

Lodging

The motel at the Hopi Cultural Center, Box 67, Second Mesa, AZ 86034, (602) 734-2401, has modern rooms with cable TV at about $55 double. Reservations are recommended.

Food

The restaurant at the **Hopi Cultural Center**, the only one on the reservation, features traditional Hopi dishes such as lamb stew, bean soup, and blue corn pancakes. Open daily from 6:30 a.m. to 9:00 p.m. in the summer months, until 8:00 p.m. the rest of the year.

About Time

The Hopi Reservation, like most of Arizona, does not observe daylight saving time. The Navajo Nation, which completely surrounds the Hopi Reservation, does. If you wanted to be sure you know the exact time, you'd need to set your watch forward an hour when entering Navajo land, then back an hour when you cross onto Hopi land; tomorrow, you'll set it forward an hour when crossing back onto Navajo land, then back an hour when you leave the reservation, and forward an hour when you enter New Mexico. Fortunately, today's and tomorrow's route is in the "Indian time" zone; what your watch says doesn't matter anyway.

THE PETRIFIED FOREST AND ZUÑI COUNTRY

This long driving day will take you through the painted desert country of eastern Arizona, then back to New Mexico in the land of the Zuñi. End your day at a place where every expedition that passed through New Mexico for 200 years left its mark in stone alongside petroglyphs of the Anasazi before them.

Suggested Schedule

9:00 a.m.	Leave for the Petrified Forest.
11:30 a.m.	Arrive at Petrified Forest National Park. See the hard woods and rainbow sands.
1:30 p.m.	Leave for El Morro.
4:30 p.m.	Arrive at El Morro National Monument. Find a campsite (or drive on to Grants for lodging tonight).

Travel Route: Second Mesa to El Morro (285 miles)
Continue on AZ 264 over First Mesa, through Keams Canyon, a total distance of 39 miles to the turnoff for Tribal Route 6, which becomes AZ 77 and goes to Holbrook, 59 miles to the south. There are no towns along this route. You will reach I-40 just east of Holbrook. After stopping in town for gasoline if necessary, proceed eastbound on I-40 for 25 miles to the Petrified Forest entrance.

After the 27-mile drive through the Petrified Forest, exit at the far end of the park on US 180 and drive 36 miles east across empty, arid rangeland to St. Johns. Turn north on US 666 and drive north for 29 miles to the turnoff for AZ 61 on your right. A few miles east, AZ 61 changes into NM 53. Stay on that road, admiring the pink cliffs of the Zuñi Mountains, for 30 miles to the town of Zuñi and about 40 more miles to El Morro National Monument.

Sightseeing Highlights

▲▲▲ **Petrified Forest National Park**—This colorful patch of apparent wasteland was a tropical forest 200 million years ago. Trees similar to California's giant redwoods grew along the shore of a sea that rose and receded over countless millennia to deposit multicolored layers of sediment, burying and petrifying parts of the forest. Wind and rain erosion have exposed the huge stone tree trunks and created the striking painted desert around them. The idea of primeval forest here, in a land where today scraggly clumps of grass struggle to survive, challenges the imagination. With the coming of the railroad in 1883, entrepreneurs began sawing and polishing petrified wood to ship back east, where it was a fashionable material for table tops. In just 16 years, they shipped out over 20 million pounds of it. To stop the plunder, Theodore Roosevelt declared the petrified forest a national monument in 1899. It was raised to national park status in 1962. The National Park Service is very serious about preventing the removal of petrified wood, and vehicles are subject to search by rangers on the way out.

The most extensive petrified forest areas are in the southern part of the park. Along the 27-mile scenic drive from the south gate on US 180 to the north gate on I-40, stop and walk through the strange landscape near the **Rainbow Forest Museum** and at the **Crystal Forest** and **Jasper Forest** turnouts. Take the three-quarter-mile paved walking trail among blue, white, and brown striped hills from the fourth turnout on the one-way loop road at **Blue Mesa**, midway through the park.

The park is open only during daylight hours. Admission is $5 per vehicle. There is no lodge or campground. Food, gasoline, and souvenirs, including lots of petrified wood imported from outside the park (keep your receipt until you leave the park), are sold at the **Painted Desert Oasis** by the visitors center at the north gate.

▲ **Zuñi Reservation**—The people who live here are classified as Pueblo Indians, although their language is

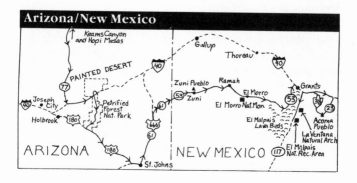

not related to that of any other known Native American tribe. They are best known for the costumed Shalako house blessing ceremonies held around the beginning of December. Now mostly of modern construction, the town of Zuñi has been continuously occupied for 700 years. Ancient ruins around Zuñi were to become Zuñi-Cibola National Historic Park under a resolution passed by the U.S. Congress in 1988. Unfortunately, nobody consulted the Zuñi people about it until 1990, when they voted the plan down. The ruins remain closed to the non-Indian public. Although it has no national park, the reservation does have some pretty little fishing lakes.

▲▲ **El Morro National Monument**—America's first national monument (1906), El Morro was established to protect the many inscriptions scratched into the sandstone around a lovely oasis at the base of the 200-foot cliffs. Though wading and bathing are prohibited, the pool looks so inviting that it's no mystery why just about every southwestern expedition for three centuries stopped here. (Besides, it was the only water for miles around.) Observe how many Spanish conquistadors, whowrotewithoutspacesbetweenwords, recorded that their journeys were "a su cuesta" (at their own expense), and note the tombstonelike precision with which U.S. military explorers inscribed their graffiti. The earliest Spanish inscription (1605) is that of Don Juan de Oñate, who led the first settlers to New Mexico. Native American petroglyphs on the same rock are twice as old.

The best part of a visit to El Morro is the one-hour loop hike to the top of the rock, where you'll find the ruins of a small Anasazi pueblo with a magnificent view. Surprise: the cliff that looks so solid and massive from below is actually a wall, 200 feet high but just a few feet thick, separating the visitors center area from a box canyon.

The visitors center and trail are open daily from 8:00 a.m. to 7:00 p.m. in the summer months, until 5:00 p.m. the rest of the year. Admission is $1 per person, maximum $3 per vehicle. While at the visitors center, pick up information sheets on nearby, undeveloped El Malpais National Monument.

Camping

El Morro has a small, pleasant campground among the juniper trees. It only fills up on weekends. There is no camping fee, though a donation box quietly solicits voluntary contributions to help pay for the new rest room.

In case you find the El Morro campground full, go to the **Inscription Rock RV Park** about a mile farther along New Mexico 53. Sites run $11 with full hookups, $8 without.

Lodging

The closest motel accommodations are one hour's drive beyond El Morro at the town of Grants on I-40. A faded uranium mining center of the 1950s, Grants exists today mainly as an overnight stop for trucks, and motel prices are low enough to convince big-rig drivers to stay here instead of rolling on into Albuquerque. Top of the line is the **Best Western Inn**, (505) 287-7901, with in-room movies, a whirlpool and sauna, and a café; doubles start at about $57. In the moderate price range, both with doubles starting around $33, are the **Holiday Inn**, (505) 287-4426, and the **Travelodge**, (505) 287-2991. There are also about a dozen ma-and-pa motels where you can get a decent room for between $15 and $20. If you're camping your way across the Southwest on a budget, you won't find a cheaper shower, real bed, and cable color TV anywhere. Look at the room first and make sure the plumbing and TV work.

Food
There is a restaurant at Petrified Forest National Park but none at El Morro. In fact, except for a small café in Zuñi, there is no food to be found along this afternoon's route. If you're camping, stock up on groceries in Holbrook or St. Johns. Otherwise, the only restaurants around are in Grants. After trying numerous family restaurants, fast-food joints, and other dining possibilities around Grants, the only place I can recommend wholeheartedly is the **Golden Skillet** coffee shop in the truck stop 3 miles west of town at the Milan exit from I-40. In case you want to place a collect or credit card phone call home, there is a telephone at each table. There are also pay showers, video games, and a store that sells cowboy hats, boots, huge belt buckles, auto repair tools, CB radios, portable sound systems, C&W cassettes, paperback westerns, soft drinks, beef jerky, silly postcards, the latest in radar detection technology—everything an interstate trucker needs.

EL MALPAIS AND ÁCOMA

The final day of your southwestern journey features the volcanic landscapes of the new El Malpais National Monument and the timeless "sky city," Ácoma Pueblo. Evening will find you back in Albuquerque, where this tour began three weeks ago.

Suggested Schedule

9:30 a.m.	Drive from El Morro to Bandera Crater and Ice Cave.
10:00 a.m.	See the ice cave and hike up to the crater.
11:30 a.m.	Take a short walk along part of the Zuñi-Ácoma Trail in El Malpais National Monument.
12:30 p.m.	Drive into Grants and have lunch.
1:30 p.m.	Take a side trip to La Ventana for the best view of El Malpais.
2:30 p.m.	Drive to Ácoma.
3:00 p.m.	Visit the old pueblo on top of the mesa.
4:30 p.m.	Drive to Albuquerque.
5:30 p.m.	Arrive back in Albuquerque.

Travel Route: El Morro to Albuquerque (150 miles)
As you continue east on NM 53 for the 40-mile drive from El Morro National Monument to Grants, watch for the little road on your right to Bandera Crater and Ice Cave, near where the highway crosses the crest of the mountains. Several miles farther along, a big brown National Park Service sign marks the trailhead for the Zuñi-Ácoma Trail.

NM 53 brings you back to I-40 at the western Grants/Milan exit. To see the other side of El Malpais, with the best views of the lava fields, take either the interstate or the business loop to the eastern Grants exit and

follow NM 117 south for 10 miles to Sandstone Bluff
Overlook and 7 more miles to La Ventana Natural Arch.
Return to the interstate by the same route.

The exit to Ácoma is 15 miles east on I-40. Albuquerque is another 60 miles down the interstate.

Sightseeing Highlights

▲▲ Bandera Crater and Ice Cave—Hike about a mile
to see Bandera Crater, one of five volcanoes that created
the El Malpais lava field. Nearby, another short trail leads
to an ice cave. The porous lava insulates an underground
pond, keeping it perpetually frozen; the cave is often 70
degrees cooler than the temperature on the surface. This
privately owned tourist attraction will become a part of
El Malpais National Monument at some future date when
the National Park Service has the funding to acquire it. In
the meantime, it is the only developed facility within the
monument. Hours are 8:00 a.m. to 7:00 p.m. during the
summer months, until 4:00 p.m. the rest of the year.
Admission is $5 for adults, $4 for children ages 5 to 11.

▲ El Malpais National Monument—Created by act of
Congress in 1988, El Malpais is one of the nation's newest
national monuments. Because of tight National Park Service budgets in recent years, there have been no improve-
ments except for a few signs. The information center, in a
former gas station at 620 E. Santa Fe Street in Grants, can
furnish photocopied flyers on hiking and show you a
map of the area. Otherwise, you're on your own. Malpais,
Spanish for "badlands," is the name given to lava beds
throughout New Mexico. Three thousand years ago, a
row of volcanoes gushed a river of molten rock 30 miles
long and up to 20 miles wide.

You can hike along the edge of the lava beds, which are
quite different from those you saw at Sunset Crater, by
taking the **Zuñi-Ácoma Trail**, a fragment of the route
that once linked the two ancient pueblos. Although
mostly level, this trail is slow and difficult because of the
rough terrain. The trail itself is indistinct, so you must follow marker posts. The marked portion of the trail runs

for 7½ miles, but the first mile may be enough.

The best view of the lava field is from the opposite side of the lava field at **Sandstone Bluff Overlook** on NM 117. From there, continue to La Ventana to see the largest accessible natural arch in New Mexico.

▲▲ **Ácoma (Sky City)**—Ácoma is the most impressively situated of New Mexico's Indian pueblos as well as one of the oldest and most traditional. Continuously inhabited since A.D. 1075 (when Chaco Canyon was at its zenith), Ácoma was one of the towns, along with Zuñi, that inspired the "Seven Cities of Cibola" legend that drew Coronado to explore the American Southwest in A.D. 1540 in search of rumored wealth surpassing that of the Incas. (Was he disappointed!) The pueblo also has a Franciscan mission church dating from 1629 (older than San Miguel, Santa Fe's "Oldest Church in the U.S."). Eighty such missions were built in the 1600s, but only two survived the Pueblo Revolt of 1680. The other is at Isleta Pueblo near Albuquerque.

While most Ácoma people now live in modern villages below the mesa, the old pueblo remains the center of religious life. Ácoma is on top of the 400-foot mesa, 13 miles by road. No cars are permitted beyond the tribal visitors center near the interstate. Access is by shuttle bus. The tours, which run hourly from 8:00 a.m. to 6:00 p.m. during the summer months (shorter hours off-season) cost $5 per adult, $3 for children ages 7 to 17. Camera and sketching permit fees are the highest of any Indian pueblo in New Mexico. The pueblo is closed for religious ceremonies to which the public is not invited on several days during the summer and fall. For current schedule information, call ahead at (505) 252-1139.

Walk in Beauty
I sincerely hope you've enjoyed your southwestern trip as much as I've enjoyed sharing this information with you. I welcome your comments, suggestions, or discoveries. Write me c/o John Muir Publications, whose address appears in the last pages of this book.

Travel beckons us with pretty places and enchanting
promises but leaves us, at the end, with experiences that
can translate into a better understanding of our world. As
you finish your southwestern trip, take a moment to think
back on the meaning of what you've seen. Nobody has
said it better than the Navajo singer of "Nahasdzaan
Shima":

Earth My Mother,
We see you dressed in beautiful colors.
Father Sky provides beautiful things to you.
Like a man gives beautiful things to his wife.
Now we use up and destroy these beautiful things.
Now we are hurt because you are hurt.
You only ask us for blessings and respect;
You only expect us to work together in balance and
*   harmony.*
Earth My Mother,
We will return to you these gifts of beauty and grace.
We will return with beauty and grace.

INDEX

Other Books from John Muir Publications

Adventure Vacations: From Trekking in New Guinea to Swimming in Siberia, Richard Bangs (65-76-9) 256 pp. $17.95

Asia Through the Back Door, 3rd ed., Rick Steves and John Gottberg (65-48-3) 326 pp. $15.95

Being a Father: Family, Work, and Self, *Mothering* Magazine (65-69-6) 176 pp. $12.95

Buddhist America: Centers, Retreats, Practices, Don Morreale (28-94-X) 400 pp. $12.95

Bus Touring: Charter Vacations, U.S.A., Stuart Warren with Douglas Bloch (28-95-8) 168 pp. $9.95

California Public Gardens: A Visitor's Guide, Eric Sigg (65-56-4) 304 pp. $16.95

Catholic America: Self-Renewal Centers and Retreats, Patricia Christian-Meyer (65-20-3) 325 pp. $13.95

Complete Guide to Bed & Breakfasts, Inns & Guesthouses, 1991-92, Pamela Lanier (65-43-2) 520 pp. $16.95

Costa Rica: A Natural Destination, Ree Strange Sheck (65-51-3) 280 pp. $15.95

Elderhostels: The Students' Choice, Mildred Hyman (65-28-9) 224 pp. $12.95 (2nd ed. available 5/91 $15.95)

Environmental Vacations: Volunteer Projects to Save the Planet, Stephanie Ocko (65-78-5) 240 pp. $15.95

Europe 101: History & Art for the Traveler, 4th ed., Rick Steves and Gene Openshaw (65-79-3) 372 pp. $15.95

Europe Through the Back Door, 9th ed., Rick Steves (65-42-4) 432 pp. $16.95

Floating Vacations: River, Lake, and Ocean Adventures, Michael White (65-32-7) 256 pp. $17.95

Gypsying After 40: A Guide to Adventure and Self-Discovery, Bob Harris (28-71-0) 264 pp. $14.95

The Heart of Jerusalem, Arlynn Nellhaus (28-79-6) 336 pp. $12.95

Indian America: A Traveler's Companion, Eagle/Walking Turtle (65-29-7) 424 pp. $16.95 (2nd ed. available 7/91 $16.95)

Mona Winks: Self-Guided Tours of Europe's Top Museums, Rick Steves and Gene Openshaw (28-85-0) 456 pp. $14.95

Opera! The Guide to Western Europe's Great Houses, Karyl Lynn Zietz (65-81-5) 280 pp. $18.95 (Available 4/91)

Paintbrushes and Pistols: How the Taos Artists Sold the West, Sherry C. Taggett and Ted Schwarz (65-65-3) 280 pp. $17.95

The People's Guide to Mexico, 8th ed., Carl Franz (65-60-2) 608 pp. $17.95

The People's Guide to RV Camping in Mexico, Carl Franz with Steve Rogers (28-91-5) 320 pp. $13.95

Preconception: A Woman's Guide to Preparing for Pregnancy and Parenthood, Brenda E. Aikey-Keller (65-44-0) 232 pp. $14.95

Ranch Vacations: The Complete Guide to Guest and Resort, Fly-Fishing, and Cross-Country Skiing Ranches, Eugene Kilgore (65-30-0) 392 pp. $18.95 (2nd ed. available 5/91 $18.95)

Schooling at Home: Parents, Kids, and Learning, *Mothering* Magazine (65-52-1) 264 pp. $14.95

The Shopper's Guide to Art and Crafts in the Hawaiian Islands, Arnold Schuchter (65-61-0) 272 pp. $13.95

The Shopper's Guide to Mexico, Steve Rogers and Tina Rosa (28-90-7) 224 pp. $9.95

Ski Tech's Guide to Equipment, Skiwear, and Accessories, edited by Bill Tanler (65-45-9) 144 pp. $11.95

Ski Tech's Guide to Maintenance and Repair, edited by Bill Tanler (65-46-7) 160 pp. $11.95

Teens: A Fresh Look, *Mothering* Magazine (65-54-8) 240 pp. $14.95

A Traveler's Guide to Asian Culture, Kevin Chambers (65-14-9) 224 pp. $13.95

Traveler's Guide to Healing Centers and Retreats in North America, Martine Rudee and Jonathan Blease (65-15-7) 240 pp. $11.95

Understanding Europeans, Stuart Miller (65-77-7) 272 pp. $14.95
Undiscovered Islands of the Caribbean, 2nd ed., Burl Willes (65-55-6) 232 pp. $14.95
Undiscovered Islands of the Mediterranean, Linda Lancione Moyer and Burl Willes (65-53-X) 232 pp. $14.95
A Viewer's Guide to Art: A Glossary of Gods, People, and Creatures, Marvin S. Shaw and Richard Warren (65-66-1) 152 pp. $10.95

2 to 22 Days Series

These pocket-size itineraries (4½" × 8") are a refreshing departure from ordinary guidebooks. Each offers 22 flexible daily itineraries that can be used to get the most out of vacations of any length. Included are not only "must see" attractions but also little-known villages and hidden "jewels" as well as valuable general information.

22 Days Around the World, Roger Rapoport and Burl Willes (65-31-9) 200 pp. $9.95 (1992 ed. available 8/91 $11.95)
2 to 22 Days Around the Great Lakes, 1991 ed., Arnold Schuchter (65-62-9) 176 pp. $9.95
22 Days in Alaska, Pamela Lanier (28-68-0) 128 pp. $7.95
22 Days in the American Southwest, 2nd ed., Richard Harris (28-88-5) 176 pp. $9.95
22 Days in Asia, Roger Rapoport and Burl Willes (65-17-3) 136 pp. $7.95 (1992 ed. available 8/91 $9.95)
22 Days in Australia, 3rd ed., John Gottberg (65-40-8) 148 pp. $7.95 (1992 ed. available 8/91 $9.95)
22 Days in California, 2nd ed., Roger Rapoport (65-64-5) 176 pp. $9.95
22 Days in China, Gaylon Duke and Zenia Victor (28-72-9) 144 pp. $7.95
22 Days in Europe, 5th ed., Rick Steves (65-63-7) 192 pp. $9.95
22 Days in Florida, Richard Harris (65-27-0) 136 pp. $7.95 (1992 ed. available 8/91 $9.95)
22 Days in France, Rick Steves (65-07-6) 154 pp. $7.95 (1991 ed. available 4/91 $9.95)
22 Days in Germany, Austria & Switzerland, 3rd ed., Rick Steves (65-39-4) 136 pp. $7.95
22 Days in Great Britain, 3rd ed., Rick Steves (65-38-6) 144 pp. $7.95 (1991 ed. available 4/91 $9.95)
22 Days in Hawaii, 2nd ed., Arnold Schuchter (65-50-5) 144 pp. $7.95 (1992 ed. available 8/91 $9.95)
22 Days in India, Anurag Mathur (28-87-7) 136 pp. $7.95
22 Days in Japan, David Old (28-73-7) 136 pp. $7.95
22 Days in Mexico, 2nd ed., Steve Rogers and Tina Rosa (65-41-6) 128 pp. $7.95
22 Days in New England, Anne Wright (28-96-6) 128 pp. $7.95 (1991 ed. available 4/91 $9.95)
2 to 22 Days in New Zealand, 1991 ed., Arnold Schuchter (65-58-0) 176 pp. $9.95
22 Days in Norway, Sweden, & Denmark, Rick Steves (28-83-4) 136 pp. $7.95 (1991 ed. available 4/91 $9.95)
22 Days in the Pacific Northwest, Richard Harris (28-97-4) 136 pp. $7.95 (1991 ed. available 4/91 $9.95)
22 Days in the Rockies, Roger Rapoport (65-68-8) 176 pp. $9.95
22 Days in Spain & Portugal, 3rd ed., Rick Steves (65-06-8) 136 pp. $7.95
22 Days in Texas, Richard Harris (65-47-5) 176 pp. $9.95
22 Days in Thailand, Derk Richardson (65-57-2) 176 pp. $9.95
22 Days in the West Indies, Cyndy Morreale and Sam Morreale (28-74-5) 136 pp. $7.95

"Kidding Around" Travel Guides for Young Readers

Written for kids eight years of age and older. Generously illustrated in two colors with imaginative characters and images. An adventure to read and a treasure to keep.

Kidding Around Atlanta, Anne Pedersen (65-35-1) 64 pp. $9.95
Kidding Around Boston, Helen Byers (65-36-X) 64 pp. $9.95
Kidding Around Chicago, Lauren Davis (65-70-X) 64 pp. $9.95
Kidding Around the Hawaiian Islands, Sarah Lovett (65-37-8) 64 pp. $9.95
Kidding Around London, Sarah Lovett (65-24-6) 64 pp. $9.95
Kidding Around Los Angeles, Judy Cash (65-34-3) 64 pp. $9.95

Kidding Around the National Parks of the Southwest, Sarah Lovett 108 pp. $12.95
Kidding Around New York City, Sarah Lovett (65-33-5) 64 pp. $9.95
Kidding Around Paris, Rebecca Clay (65-82-3) 64 pp. $9.95 (Available 4/91)
Kidding Around Philadelphia, Rebecca Clay (65-71-8) 64 pp. $9.95
Kidding Around San Francisco, Rosemary Zibart (65-23-8) 64 pp. $9.95
Kidding Around Santa Fe, Susan York (65-99-8) 64 pp. $9.95 (Available 5/91)
Kidding Around Seattle, Rick Steves (65-84-X) 64 pp. $9.95 (Available 4/91)
Kidding Around Washington, D.C., Anne Pedersen (65-25-4) 64 pp. $9.95

Environmental Books for Young Readers

Written for kids eight years and older. Examines the environmental issues and opportunities that today's kids will face during their lives.

The Indian Way: Learning to Communicate with Mother Earth, Gary McLain (65-73-4) 114 pp. $9.95
The Kids' Environment Book: What's Awry and Why, Anne Pedersen (55-74-2) 192 pp. $13.95
Rads, Ergs, and Cheeseburgers: The Kids' Guide to Energy and the Environment, Bill Yanda (65-75-0) 108 pp. $12.95

"Extremely Weird" Series for Young Readers

Written for kids eight years of age and older. Designed to help kids appreciate the world around them. Each book includes full-color photographs with detailed and entertaining descriptions.

Extremely Weird Bats, Sarah Lovett (61-008-2) 48 pp. $9.95 paper (Available 6/91)
Extremely Weird Frogs, Sarah Lovett (61-006-6) 48 pp. $9.95 paper (Available 6/91)
Extremely Weird Spiders, Sarah Lovett (61-007-4) 48 pp. $9.95 paper (Available 6/91)

Automotive Repair Manuals

How to Keep Your VW Alive, 14th ed., (65-80-7) 440 pp. $19.95
How to Keep Your Subaru Alive (65-11-4) 480 pp. $19.95
How to Keep Your Toyota Pickup Alive (28-81-3) 392 pp. $19.95
How to Keep Your Datsun/Nissan Alive (28-65-6) 544 pp. $19.95

Other Automotive Books

The Greaseless Guide to Car Care Confidence: Take the Terror Out of Talking to Your Mechanic, Mary Jackson (65-19-X) 224 pp. $14.95

Off-Road Emergency Repair & Survival, James Ristow (65-26-2) 160 pp. $9.95

Ordering Information

If you cannot find our books in your local bookstore, you can order directly from us. Please check the "Available" date above. If you send us money for a book not yet available, we will hold your money until we can ship you the book. Your books will be sent to you via UPS (for U.S. destinations). UPS will not deliver to a P.O. Box; please give us a street address. Include $2.75 for the first item ordered and $.50 for each additional item to cover shipping and handling costs. For airmail within the U.S., enclose $4.00. All foreign orders will be shipped surface rate; please enclose $3.00 for the first item and $1.00 for each additional item. Please inquire about foreign airmail rates.

Method of Payment

Your order may be paid by check, money order, or credit card. We cannot be responsible for cash sent through the mail. All payments must be made in U.S. dollars drawn on a U.S. bank. Canadian postal money orders in U.S. dollars are acceptable. For VISA, MasterCard, or American Express orders, include your card number, expiration date, and your signature, or call (800) 888-7504. Books ordered on American Express cards can be shipped only to the billing address of the cardholder. Sorry, no C.O.D.'s. Residents of sunny New Mexico, add 5.875% tax to the total.

Address all orders and inquiries to:

John Muir Publications
P.O. Box 613
Santa Fe, NM 87504
(505) 982-4078
(800) 888-7504